Cierra Block

LONDON
BLOCK by BLOCK

To Clemmie,
my darling girl who is
always up for an adventure.

Cierra Block

LONDON
BLOCK by BLOCK

OH EDITIONS

London block by block

CONTENTS

PART THREE

London by Interest 101

PART FOUR

London by Season 143

I 'm Cierra and I love creating illustrations to inspire your next adventure. I have lived in London since 2013 and I am so glad I get to call it home. I love all that London has to offer – I can't get enough of the food, history, culture, events, theatre, shopping, beautiful buildings and gardens. It's no wonder people fall in love with London, whether they are visiting for a weekend or have lived here their entire lives.

I created London Block by Block as a way to organise my favourite things about London. I wanted to create guides that are highly visual and fun but that also provide helpful information. Every map I create starts with an idea. It might be, Where are the best pancakes in London? What are the places everyone should visit in Marylebone? Or, Where in London

can you lose hours browsing the shelves of a beautiful bookshop? From there I research and curate a list to create a useful guide. Doing map research is one of my favourite aspects of my job. I spend hours walking around neighbourhoods, sitting in coffee shops, perusing shops, trying new-to-me bakeries and cafes, and looking for hidden corners. I am constantly consulting my ever-growing library of books about London, from history to fiction, kids books to cookbooks and everything in between. I also find a lot of inspiration from the internet. I love reading blogs about London, browsing Instagram looking for inspiration and reading articles about all the goings on.

The next step is creating the map. This is always the most exciting part for me. I love playing around with how best to visually represent each element to make the perfect map. My goal is to create illustrations that are both beautiful and useful, that can be used as a guide for a day out in London or framed and hung as a piece of art in your home. Ultimately I want to produce beautiful maps that allow people to create memorable experiences of one of the best cities in the world.

Humans have been using maps for thousands of years. When we look at a map we can make sense of our surroundings; we intuitively understand the relationship between where we are and where we want to go. The joy of creating my maps is that they are artistic and lovely to look at but also offer functionality and utility. And all the better if they lead you to a hidden corner of London or a delicious bakery!

In this book, I hope you find some inspiration, whether it's your first visit, you're a seasoned vacationer or an all-your-life local. That's the wonderful thing about London: there's always more to explore.

Cierra x

LONDON

BY FOOD

PART ONE

AFTERNOON TEA + CHOCOLATE + PANCAKES + CHEESE LOVERS

+ COFFEE SHOPS + LONDON PUBS + FOOD MARKETS + HOT CHOCOLATE

+ ICE CREAM + BAKERIES

Brigit's Bakery

The Langham

Cutter & Squidge

Rosewood

Sketch

The Savoy

The Orangerie

Cakes & Bubbles

The Connaught

Claridge's

Fortnum & Mason

The Kensington

The Berkley

Peggy Porschen

The Ampersand

AFTERNOON TEA

LONDON BY FOOD

One indulgence I'd highly recommend when visiting London is afternoon tea. Invented around 180 years ago, afternoon tea is a delicious part of *British culture* that is enjoyed by both tourists and locals alike. From *top pastry chefs* at five-star hotels to *local bakeries,* you really can take your pick of where to enjoy your tea. Regardless of where you go, the formula is almost always the same. Little sandwiches, fresh scones with clotted cream and jam, indulgent sweet treats and delicious tea – it will be a true *event to remember.* From traditional to child-friendly and casual to avant garde, there is an afternoon tea out there for everyone.

The Berkley

Wilton Pl, SW1X 7RL The Prêt-à-Portea afternoon tea features style icons you can eat.

The Orangerie at Kensington Palace

Kensington Gardens, W8 4PX The only place in London where you can enjoy afternoon tea in the grounds of a royal palace.

The Kensington Hotel

113 Queen's Gate, SW7 5LP London landmarks have been turned into mouth-watering desserts, including a lemon curd Big Ben, a carrot cake Shard and a dark chocolate Gherkin.

The Ampersand Hotel

Harrington Rd, SW7 3ER If you love an interactive experience the Science Afternoon Tea is for you. The perfect way to unwind after spending a day at the museums.

Brigit's Bakery

6–7 Chandos Pl, WC2N 4HU Enjoy afternoon tea while seeing the sites of London on an old Routemaster bus.

The Connaught

Carlos Pl, W1K 2AL An indulgent afternoon tea in the heart of Mayfair.

Cutter & Squidge

Brewer St, W1F 0SJ Test out your magical abilities and take afternoon tea in The Potions Room.

Cakes and Bubbles

70 Regent St, W1B 4DY Unique artisan desserts in the heart of Piccadilly.

Peggy Porschen

Multiple locations, Belgravia, Chelsea This iconic pink London cafe offers a delicious afternoon tea.

Fortnum & Mason

181 Piccadilly, W1A 1ER Enjoy tea in the Diamond Jubilee Tea Salon, opened by the Queen herself, at this iconic London destination. **(GF, DF, VEG available)**

The Langham

1 Portland Pl, W1B 1JA With a focus on local and seasonal ingredients, the Palm Court is a delight. They also have an enchanting children's afternoon tea if you are looking for a special day out with the kids.

Rosewood London

252 High Holborn, WC1V 7EN A contemporary afternoon tea is inspired by some of the greatest artists. Each dessert is a mini art piece in itself and are almost too beautiful to eat.

Claridge's

Brook Street, W1K 4HR A seasonally changing menu with special menus for every holiday. With a focus on British ingredients, this afternoon tea is one that is sure to delight.

Sketch

9 Conduit St, W1S 2XG Enjoy tea in THAT pink room. It will not disappoint – from the food to the service, everything is top notch.

The Savoy

Strand, WC2R 0EZ Having served afternoon tea since 1889, they are masters in tradition. The sweeping view of the Thames and five-star service makes the experience extra special.

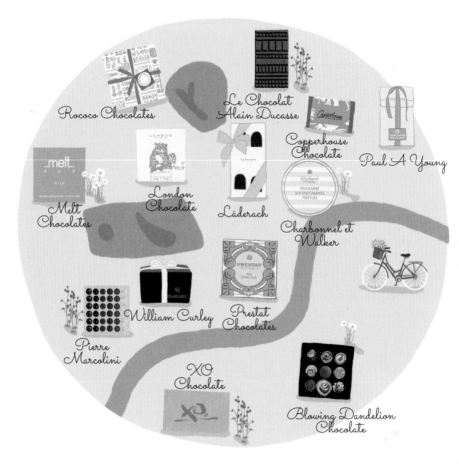

Rococo Chocolates

Le Chocolat
Alain Ducasse

Copperhouse
Chocolate

Paul A Young

Melt
Chocolates

London
Chocolate

Läderach

Charbonnel et
Walker

William Curley

Prestat
Chocolates

Pierre
Marcolini

XO
Chocolate

Blowing Dandelion
Chocolate

CHOCOLATE

Before the Industrial Revolution chocolate was something that was laborious, time intensive and *very expensive* to make. This meant it was not something enjoyed by everyday people. But advances to mechanization in the late 1800s meant chocolate could be mass produced and, more importantly, enjoyed by the masses. It was still considered a *luxury*, but one that people could afford for special occasions and holidays. We still enjoy these *seasonal delights* today, from chocolate boxes on Valentine's to chocolate eggs at Easter, and chocolate everything at Christmas. Master chocolatiers around London are serving up chocolate in all its shapes and forms, for every occasion. From bean to bar to *handmade truffles*, there is something sure to please everyone at these incredible chocolate shops.

Melt Chocolates

59 Ledbury Rd, W11 2AA Handmade in Notting Hill with offerings of freshly made chocolates, brownies, hot cocoa and chocolate bars.

Rococo Chocolates

Multiple locations across London Delicious flavours and all manner of chocolate delights, from truffles to scorched almonds to chocolate bars in an array of flavours.

Charbonnel et Walker

The Royal Arcade, Old Bond St, W1S 4BT One of England's oldest chocolatiers, with classic flavours and beautiful packaging. Holding a royal warrant, they have been a favourite of the royals since 1875.

London Chocolate

17 Connaught St, W2 2AY Small-batch bean-to-bar chocolates made in the heart of Connaught Village. You can book a tour of the bean-to-bar process in their shop and see how the chocolate is made.

Prestat Chocolates

14 Princes Arcade, SW1Y 6DS You can't go wrong with a lovely box of chocolates from royal-warrant-holding Prestat.

Paul A Young

Multiple locations, SOHO, Islington Award-winning chocolatier Paul Young has two shops in London selling beautifully crafted chocolates that are sure to delight.

Pierre Marcolini

Multiple locations, Marylebone, Harrods, Selfridges Belgian chocolate at its finest. Innovation and sustainability are key to the chocolate-making process at Pierre Marcolini.

Le Chocolat Alain Ducasse

Coal Drops Yard, 15 Bagley Walk, N1C 4DH Handcrafted bean to bar chocolate made in the heart of Paris. This luxurious French chocolate has found a warm welcome in London.

Läderach

254 Regent St, W1B 3AA For 60 years Läderach has been producing the finest chocolates in the Swiss Alps. This central London outpost offers up all of their delightful chocolate creations, without you having to travel to Switzerland.

Copperhouse Chocolate

1 Chapel Market, N1 9EZ Unparalleled vegan hot chocolate, chocolates, brownies and baked goods are all lovingly made in this North London cafe.

William Curley

Multiple locations, Soho, Harrods Award-winning chocolates made using the finest ingredients. They also make delicious macarons, biscuits and cakes.

XO Chocolate

Chocolate London 87 Quicks Rd, SW19 1EX Stunning chocolates handcrafted into mini masterpieces that are almost too pretty to eat. But do eat them because they are divine.

Blowing Dandelion Chocolate

3 Belvedere Rd, SE19 2HJ Chocolate cake, truffles and, their real star, the Chocolate Solar System are loving handcrafted at this South London chocolaterie.

Greenberry

Electric Diner

Le Creperie de
Hampstead

Millfields

Fuwa
Fuwa

Half Cup

Proud Mary's

Chiltern Fire
House

Farm Girl

Riding House
Cafe

The
Breakfast
Club

Outsider Tart

Granger
and Co

Where the
Pancakes Are

The Wolseley

Little Blue Door

Flotsam and Jepsam

Milk

PANCAKES

Enjoying a stack of pancakes is the perfect way to start any day. In London, you can find just about *every type* of pancake available, from *American-style buttermilk* pancakes and *traditional French crêpes* to fluffy Japanese pancakes and mouthwatering ricotta hotcakes. There are delicious pancakes to be found in *every corner of London,* so if you are looking for some of the best pancakes this city has to offer then look no further.

Flotsam and Jepsam

4 Bellevue Parade, SW17 7EQ American-style pancakes served swimming in syrup, topped with bacon, berries and marscapone!

Chiltern Fire House

1 Chiltern St, W1U 7PA Fluffy buttermilk pancakes cooked to perfection and served with berries.

Electric Diner

191 Portobello Rd, W11 2ED Classic American-style pancakes with whipped butter and maple syrup.

Farm Girl

59A Portobello Rd, W11 3DB Try the 'Cherry Ripe', a buttermilk buckwheat pancake with coconut, cherry and chocolate on top!

Fuwa Fuwa

37 Pembridge Rd, W11 3HG Here you can get Japanese soufflé pancakes that are as light as air and with that perfect wobble. They also come with a range of tasty toppings.

Granger and Co

Multiple locations, Chelsea, Clerkenwell, King's Cross, Notting Hill Super light ricotta hotcakes with banana, maple syrup and melted honeycomb butter.

Greenberry

101 Regent's Park Rd, NW1 8UR Buttermilk pancakes served with ricotta and berries.

Half Cup

100–102 Judd St, WC1H 9NT A savoury stack full of melted cheese, Parma ham and topped with a fried egg

Le Creperie de Hampstead

77 Hampstead High St, NW3 1RE The most authentic French crepes you'll find in London.

Little Blue Door

871–873 Fulham Rd, SW6 5HP Saturday brunch sorted. Pancakes with charred fruit, sour cream and honey.

The Breakfast Club

12–16 Artillery Lane, E1 7LS American pancakes and classic breakfast foods served with plenty of syrup.

Outsider Tart

83 Chiswick High Rd, W4 2EF Pick between buttermilk and cornmeal pancakes, served with berries and American hospitality.

Proud Mary's

1C Oaklands Grove, W12 0JD A large stack of super-thick pancakes served with a generous side of syrup and lots of berries and banana.

Riding House Cafe

43–51 Great Titchfield St, W1W 7PQ Indulgent blueberry buttermilk pancakes topped with clotted cream and lots of maple syrup.

The Wolseley

160 Piccadilly, W1J 9EB Some of London's most photographed pancakes, and it's easy to see why. They also offer classic crepes too.

Where the Pancakes Are

85A Southwark Bridge Rd, SE1 0NQ Something for everyone, from classic buttermilk pancakes to Dutch Babies.

Milk

18–20 Bedford Hill, SW12 9RG Pancakes are an ever-changing special on their weekend brunch menu; they always make use of more unusual ingredients.

Millfields

145 Chatsworth Rd, E5 0LA One extra-large delicious pancake covered with cream cheese, edible flowers and fresh fruit.

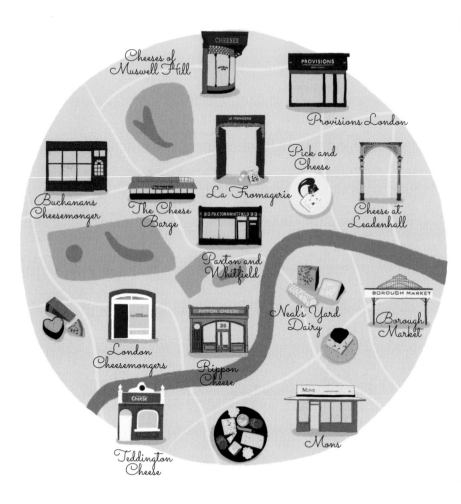

Cheeses of Muswell Hill

Provisions London

La Fromagerie

Pick and Cheese

Buchanans Cheesemonger

The Cheese Barge

Cheese at Leadenhall

Paxton and Whitfield

Neal's Yard Dairy

Borough Market

London Cheesemongers

Rippon Cheese

Teddington Cheese

Mons

CHEESE LOVERS

LONDON BY FOOD

The UK has a long (and delicious) cheese history. Celts created something akin to cottage cheese, the *Romans* brought techniques with them to create hard cheese, French monks crafted cheese in *rural monasteries*, and today artisan dairy farms are creating new flavours. The UK's rich history with cheese is something to be *celebrated*, and then tasted.

At cheese shops around London you can find the best British and continental cheeses on offer. From *Cheddar* to Cornish yarg, Brie to bergfichte, mild to robust and hard to soft, there is *something for everyone*. The cheesemongers in London are *passionate* and knowledgeable, and I've found they're always happy to talk about the cheese as well as help pick the *perfect cheese* for any occasion. I always ask what cheese they are enjoying at that moment, and I've discovered some great cheeses that I probably wouldn't have picked if left to my own devices.

Cheese at Leadenhall

4–5 Leadenhall Market, EC3V 1LR A cheese-and-small-plates cafe located in the iconic and beautiful Leadenhall Market.

Buchanans Cheesemonger

5A Porchester Pl, W2 2BS A charming cheese shop in the heart of Connaught Village. They source UK and European cheeses and the friendly staff will happily help you find the perfect cheese.

Cheeses of Muswell Hill

13 Fortis Green Rd, N10 3HP This beautifully curated family-run cheese shop sources artisan and farmhouse cheeses from around the world and sells over 200 different types.

Paxton and Whitfield

Multiple locations, St James, Chelsea This 225-year-old cheese shop currently holds two royal warrants (one for the Queen and one for the Prince of Wales) and used to be the official royal cheesemonger to Queen Victoria.

Borough Market

Borough Market, SE1 9DE Home to many delicious food vendors and delicious cheese stalls. Some favourites are Borough Cheese Company, Kappacasein Dairy and Jumi Cheese.

Mons Cheesemongers

Multiple locations, East Dulwich, Bermondsey, Borough Market, Brockley Market A beautiful selection of traditionally crafted continental and British cheeses.

Rippon Cheese

26 Upper Tachbrook Street, SW1V 1SW This family-run business offers over 500 different varieties of cheese from across Europe.

Teddington Cheese
Multiple locations, Teddington, Richmond Cheeses on offer here are sourced from small farms using traditional methods.

London Cheesemongers
251 Pavilion Rd, SW1X 0BP This small shop stocks a beautifully curated selection of cheese that changes seasonally.

Provisions London
167 Holloway Rd, N7 8LX Specializing in raw milk cheese and natural wines from Europe, as well a lovely deli section.

The Cheese Barge
Sheldon Square, W2 6DL A floating barge on the Regent's Canal in Paddington serving up everything cheesey.

Pick and Cheese
Seven Dials Market, Short's Gardens, WC2H 9AT A cheese conveyor belt restaurant in Covent Garden Market. Pick your fancy.

La Fromagerie
Multiple locations, Marylebone, Bloomsbury, Highbury Dine in or get your cheese to go. They also do supper clubs and cheese-tasting nights.

Neal's Yard Dairy
Multiple locations, Covent Garden, Borough Market, Islington
Neal's Yard works with cheesemakers across the British Isles to serve up the best British cheeses.

Intermission
Coffee

Redemption
Roasters

Attendant

Ozone
Coffee

Over
Under

The
Monocle
Cafe

Monmouth
Coffee

Omotesando

Watch
House

Rossalyn

Kiss the Hippo

Formative

Arabica

Prufrock

The Gentlemen
Baristas

Antipode

Story Coffee

Federation

COFFEE SHOPS

Tea isn't the only drink on the menu in London. In fact, London has no shortage of *amazing coffee*. Every pocket of the city has its own coffee shops, roasters and brewers that are *passionate* about their craft. Whether you are looking to grab your morning coffee, a quick pick-me-up or you're *going on a first date*, here are some of the best coffee shops you can visit in London. And if you can't make it to London, several of these shops sell their *blends* online.

Antipode

28 Fulham Palace Rd, W6 9PH Cafe by day serving up Square Mile coffee and bar by night serving wine, beer and cocktails.

Arabica

Multiple locations, Covent Garden, Mayfair Passionate about the perfect coffee.

Attendant

Multiple locations across London Coffee is roasted in-house and served alongside delicious breakfasts and lunches.

Federation

Unit 77–78, Brixton Village, Coldharbour Ln, SW9 8PS
Serving up Curve Roasters coffee in eclectic and vibrant Brixton Village.

Formative

4 Butler Pl, SW1H 0RH No-nonsense coffee in the heart of Westminster. Serving up coffee weekdays only.

Intermission Coffee

The Hardy Building, Heritage Ln, NW6 2BR Sustainability is just as important as taste at Intermission.

Kiss the Hippo

Multiple locations, Richmond, Fitzrovia London's first carbon-negative company with over half a dozen blends to choose from.

Monmouth Coffee

Multiple locations, Covent Garden, Borough Market, Spa Terminus
Roasting and brewing coffee since the 1970s, Monmouth is an iconic London coffee shop.

Omotesando

8 Newman St, W1T 1PB Japanese-inspired coffee with artisanship, craftsmanship and hospitality at the core.

Over Under
Multiple locations across London Coffee and brunch by day and a cocktail bar by night.

Ozone Coffee
Multiple locations, Shoreditch, London Fields Coffee roasters and a delicious eatery.

Prufrock
23–25 Leather Ln, EC1N 7TE Bespoke coffee and a seasonal menu serving up breakfast and lunch.

Redemption Roasters
Multiple locations across London Coffee with a mission. Redemption Roasters help young offenders by training them as baristas.

Rossalyn
Multiple locations in The City Coffee and baked goods made to perfection.

Story Coffee
Multiple locations in Southwest London Coffee and brunch with quality at the core.

The Gentlemen Baristas
Multiple locations across London Coffee, pastries and brunch served in a cosy atmosphere.

The Monocle Cafe
18 Chiltern St, W1U 7QA Pastries and coffee are served up in this quaint Marylebone shop.

Watch House
Multiple locations across London Modern coffee and lovely meals on offer.

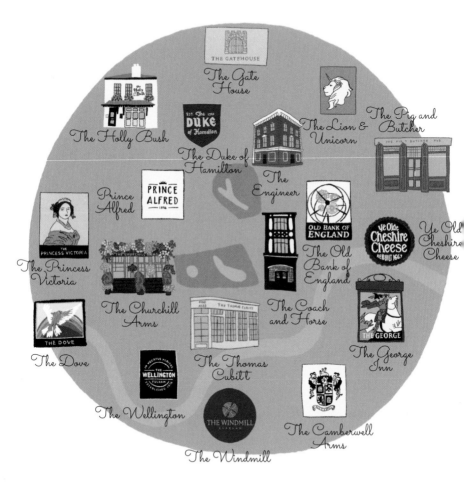

The Gate House

The Holly Bush

The Duke of Hamilton

The Lion & Unicorn

The Pig and Butcher

Prince Alfred

The Engineer

The Princess Victoria

The Old Bank of England

Ye Old Cheshire Cheese

The Churchill Arms

The Coach and Horse

The George Inn

The Dove

The Thomas Cubitt

The Wellington

The Windmill

The Camberwell Arms

LONDON PUBS

Pubs are quintessentially British. They are a place to meet, drink, eat, see friends, hang out, participate in a pub quiz, listen to music or see a fringe show.

London pubs are *something special*. Some of the oldest pubs in London were frequented by literary greats such as *Shakespeare and Dickens*. Newer pubs boast top chefs and exciting menus, serving delicious meals as well as drinks.

Whether it is a *Sunday roast* with the family, fish and chips with friends or a *romantic meal* at a gastro pub, you have countless options.

The Pig and Butcher

80 Liverpool Rd, N1 0QD An Islington institution that butchers their own rare-breeds of meat on site.

The Thomas Cubitt

44 Elizabeth St, SW1W 9PA This gastro pub is a neighbourhood favourite.

The Duke of Hamilton

23–25 New End, NW3 1JD Hampstead gastropub with a jazz club in the basement.

The Engineer

65 Gloucester Ave, Chalk Farm, NW1 8JD Charming pub in the heart of Primrose Hill with great food and atmosphere.

The Camberwell Arms

65 Camberwell Church St, SE5 8TR This gastropub is a great spot for Sunday lunch.

The Windmill

Clapham Common South Side, SW4 9DE Hotel and pub serving up British classics.

The Wellington

56 Haldane Rd, SW6 7EU British classics are served alongside craft beer and gin.

Ye Old Cheshire Cheese

145 Fleet St, EC4A 2BP Rebuilt after the Great Fire in 1666, this pub is steeped in history.

The George Inn

75 Borough High St, SE1 1NH This Grade I-listed pub has been a mainstay since before the time of Shakespeare.

Prince Alfred

5A Formosa St, W9 1EE Victorian pub with great food and a cosy atmosphere.

The Princess Victoria

217 Uxbridge Rd, W12 9DH Classic British food served in a former gin palace.

The Churchill Arms

119 Kensington Church St, W8 7LN Covered with flowers and serving up Thai food, this cosy pub is always a crowd-pleaser.

The Coach and Horse

5 Bruton St, W1J 6PT Charming and quaint inside and out. The perfect place to rest up after shopping in Mayfair.

The Old Bank of England

194 Fleet St, EC4A 2LT A stunning pub with dramatic interiors, and their garden has its own double-decker bus.

The Holly Bush

22 Holly Mount, NW3 6SG Iconic Hampstead pub with a cosy atmosphere serving up classic dishes.

The Dove

19 Upper Mall, W6 9TA Serving up good food alongside the Thames.

The Lion & Unicorn

42–44 Gaisford St, NW5 2ED Home of the Camden Fringe Festival, and serving up classic pub fare.

The Gate House

1 North Rd, N6 4BD Charming Highgate pub with tasty food and fringe theatre.

Camden Market

Netil Market

Columbia Road
Flower Market

Canopy
Market

Leadenhall
Market

Portobello Road
Market

Seven
Dials
Market

Spitalfields
Market

Brick Lane
Market

Covent Garden
Market

Greenwich
Market

Borough
Market

Duke of York
Market

Southbank
Food Market

Spa Terminus
Market

Maltby Street
Market

FOOD MARKETS

For millennium markets have been an important part of London life. Today, there are many markets across London and they are a *wonderful way to explore* and experience different areas. From food to flowers and antiques to art, there are amazing markets selling everything under the sun. One of my favourite ways to spend a weekend is exploring the *eclectic markets* dotted across the city.

I love grabbing lunch and stocking up on cheese and baked goods at Borough Market, perusing the antique stalls along Portobello Road and buying flowers on Columbia Road. They each offer up a *unique view* of London, and this traditional way of buying and selling has remained strong throughout the centuries.

Camden Market

Camden Lock Place, NW1 8AF Open daily Go for Baba G's, stay for Chin Chin Labs' desserts.

Netil Market

23 Westgate St, E8 3RL Open daily Go for Bao London, stay for The Treats Club.

Columbia Road Flower Market

Columbia Rd, E2 7RG Sundays only Go for the flowers, stay for Lily Vanilli Bakery.

Greenwich Market

Greenwich Market, SE10 9HZ Open daily Go for the world heritage sites, stay for the Andes Empanadas.

Covent Garden Market

Covent Garden, WC2E 8BU Open daily Go for Arabica, stay for Bageriet.

Seven Dials Market

35 Earlham St, WC2H 9LD Open daily Go for Pick and Cheese, stay for Yum Bun.

Spitalfields Market

56 Brushfield St, E1 6AA Open daily Go for the Arts Market, stay for Humble Crumble.

Leadenhall Market

Gracechurch St, EC3V 1LT Open daily Go for the history and stunning architecture, stay for the chocolate brioche from Aux Merveilleux de Fred.

Canopy Market

West Handyside Canopy, N1C 4BH Friday, Saturday, Sunday Go for The Big Melt, stay for Churros Garcia.

Brick Lane Market

146 Brick Ln, E1 6QL Weekends Go for the Sunday Upmarket, stay for the Backyard Market.

Borough Market

8 Southwark St, SE1 1TL Open daily Go for the Bread Ahead doughnuts, stay for Kappacasein's raclette, Padella pasta, Tacos Padre and more.

Southbank Food Market

Southbank Centre, Belvedere Rd, SE1 8XX Friday, Saturday, Sunday Go for Horn OK Please, stay for Choco Fruit and Crêpes à la carte.

Duke of York Market

80 Duke of York Square, SW3 4LY Saturdays Go for the the Dumpling Van, stay for the The Cake Hole.

Maltby Street Market

Ropewalk, Maltby St, SE1 3PA Weekends Go for The Beefsteaks, stay for the Gyoza Guys.

Spa Terminus Market

Dockley Road, SE16 3SF Some Traders open daily, full market on Saturday Go for the Little Bread Pedlar, stay for the Ice Cream Union.

Portobello Road Market

Portobello Rd, W10 5TY
Full market Saturday and Sunday, shops open daily
Go for the antiques, stay for Buns From Home.

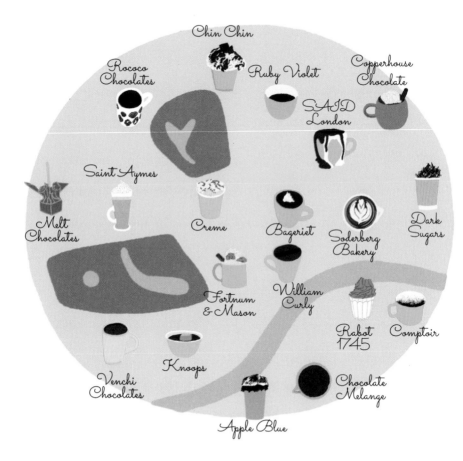

Chin Chin

Rococo
Chocolates

Ruby Violet

Copperhouse
Chocolate

SAID
London

Saint Aymes

Melt
Chocolates

Creme

Bageriet

Soderberg
Bakery

Dark
Sugars

Fortnum
& Mason

William
Curly

Rabot
1745

Comptoir

Venchi
Chocolates

Knoops

Chocolate
Melange

Apple Blue

HOT CHOCOLATE

LONDON BY FOOD

London has been at the heart of refining and crafting hot chocolate since it became a *fashionable drink* among the Georgian elite. The royals loved hot chocolate so much they even had a *chocolate kitchen* installed in Hampton Court Palace, complete with their own personal chocolatier.

Hot chocolate has come a long way since the Georgian era, and thankfully we don't need a personal chocolatier as there are *bountiful cafes* offering up this decadent drink across the city. Each of these cafes has their own unique take on hot chocolate, be it thick, thin, vegan, pink, light or dark – it's best to *try them all* and decide which is your favourite.

Apple Blue
212 Balham High Rd, SW12 9BS Thick and decadent, the hot chocolate here is more of a dessert than a drink.

Bageriet
24 Rose St, WC2E 9EA Perfect for a little escape from the hustle and bustle of Covent Garden.

Creme
4 D'Arblay St, W1F 8DJ Known for their cookies, but the hot cocoa is just as luxurious.

Chin Chin
Multiple locations, Camden, Soho For when you want to remember how awesome your school science class, with added delicious hot cocoa.

Chocolate Melange

2 Maxted Rd, SE15 4LL Decadent hot cocoa prepared with love.

Comptoir Gourmand
Multiple locations, Borough, Soho, Bermondsey, Maltby St. For when you can't decide between hot chocolate and baked goods (just get both).

Copperhouse Chocolate
1 Chapel Market, N1 9EZ For unparalleled vegan hot chocolate.

Dark Sugars
141 Brick Ln, Bethnal Green, E1 6SB For when you want all the chocolate.

Fortnum & Mason
181 Piccadilly, St. James's, W1A 1ER Perfect for when you want a sense of tradition and a bit of indulgence.

Knoops
Multiple locations across London You can pick your pleasure here, with a huge variety of hot chocolates on offer. Always go for the marshmallows.

Ruby Violet

3 Wharf Road, N1C 4BZ Ice cream parlours serve up some of the best hot cocoa.

Soderberg Bakery

36 Berwick St, W1F 8RR The cardamom hot chocolate is the perfect companion for their cinnamon buns.

Melt Chocolates

Multiple locations, Notting Hill, Holland Park For when you need a decadent hot cocoa.

Rabot 1745

2–4 Bedale St, SE1 9AL For a quick hot cocoa break while eating your way through Borourgh Market.

Rococo Chocolates

Multiple locations Across London For lovers of thick hot cocoa and dark chocolate.

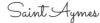

SAID London

Multiple locations, Soho, Fitzrovia Perfect for those who don't colour inside the lines and always fill their cup to the tippy top.

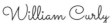

Saint Aymes

59 Connaught St, St George's Fields, W2 2BB Ever wanted a pink hot chocolate? This is your place.

Venchi Chocolates

Multiple locations, Hampstead, Covent Garden, South Kensington, Chelsea Perfect for those who can't decide between gelato and hot cocoa.

William Curly

33 Smith's Ct, W1D 7LR For when you need to get away from the hustle and bustle of Piccadilly Circus.

Chin
Chin
Labs

Mamasons Dirty
Ice Cream

Unico

Bake

Udderlicious

Gelateria
3 Bis

La Gelatiera

Gelupo

Soft Serve
Society

Milk
Train

Fortnum &
Mason

Greedy Goat
Ice Cream

Oddono's

Ice Cream
Union

ICE CREAM

You don't need to wait for the handful of hot days a year to enjoy the *delicious ice creams* on offer in London. This family-friendly treat is available year round and in many forms, from macaroon ice cream sandwiches to *liquid nitrogen* ice cream, and with an endless variety of flavours. For a country that prides itself on its dairy, it is no wonder that we are *spoiled for choice* when it comes to ice cream.

Gelateria 3 Bis

Multiple locations, Portobello Road, Borough Market This is the London outpost of an Italian original. I'm a sucker for chocolate and pistachio and I always say yes to a sprinkle cone.

Unico

Multiple locations, St John's Wood, Bromley No matter which location you go to, the due torri, salted caramel and vegan dark chocolate are all delicious.

Oddono's

Multiple locations, Chiswick, Kensington, Hampstead, Stoke Newington, East Dulwich, Wimbledon, Battersea The pistachio is definitely worth a taste.

Chin Chin Labs

Multiple locations, Camden, Soho Burnt butter caramel or valrhona chocolate. Be sure to top it with a torched marshmallow or the fleur de sel caramel sauce.

Fortnum & Mason

181 Piccadilly, W1A 1ER If you are looking for something a bit fancier than just a scoop of ice cream, the sundaes here are a smile-inducing indulgence. The original dusty road is scrumptious, as is the banana split.

Gelupo

7 Archer St, W1D 7AU Try the blood orange or honeycomb.

Bake

9 Wardour St, W1D 6PF A Japanese taiyaki cone with your choice of matcha, vanilla or a twist, because you have always wanted to eat ice cream out of a fish.

La Gelatiera

Multiple locations, Covent Garden, OXO Tower, Crouch End, Stratford They have ever-changing seasonal flavours that are very interesting. When you go here be daring and try something new.

Milk Train

12 Tavistock St, WC2E 7PH Candy floss and soft serve ice cream – the ultimate Instagrammable treat.

Udderlicious

Multiple locations, Islington, Seven Dials You have to try the dark chocolate sea salt sorbet. If I am close to an Udderlicious I will almost always stop in, no matter the season, for a scoop of this deliciousness.

Soft Serve Society

Multiple locations, Victoria, Shoreditch Get the charcoal and coconut. You probably never thought you'd want to eat black ice cream, but you would be wrong. Oh, and top it with a toasted marshmallow.

Greedy Goat Ice Cream

Borough Market, SE1 9AL Delicious goat milk ice cream situated in lovely Borough Market.

Ice Cream Union

166 Pavilion Rd, SW1X 0AW Created using top ingredients and seasonal fruits. You can't go wrong here.

Mamasons Dirty Ice Cream

Multiple locations, Camden, China Town Filipino flavours that will intrigue and delight. I'm partial to the Ube (purple yam).

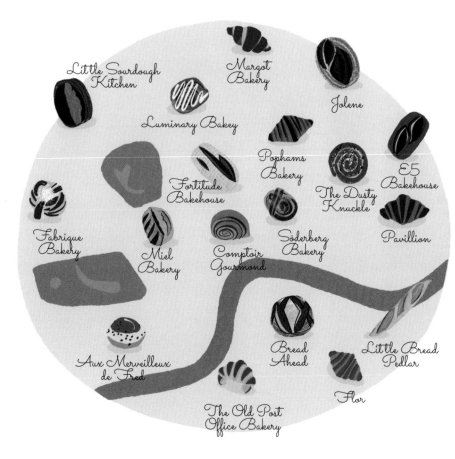

Little Sourdough
Kitchen

Margot
Bakery

Jolene

Luminary Bakey

Pophams
Bakery

E5
Bakehouse

Fortitude
Bakehouse

The Dusty
Knuckle

Fabrique
Bakery

Pavillion

Miel
Bakery

Comptoir
Gourmond

Söderberg
Bakery

Aux Merveilleux
de Fred

Bread
Ahead

Little Bread
Pedlar

Flor

The Old Post
Office Bakery

BAKERIES

Nothing quite beats slicing open a fresh loaf of bread. The crack of the crust, the *heavenly smell* of warm dough and the perfect springy texture. Thankfully London has no shortage of bakeries producing *delicious breads* and treats, from cinnamon buns to sourdough and croissants to kouign amann. You can find *artisan bakeries* in every corner of London, so whether you are looking for a fresh loaf to go with your homemade soup, a focaccia to make the *dream sandwich* or a chocolate brioche to start your weekend, London has the *perfect bakery* for you, if you just know where to look.

Little Sourdough Kitchen

237 Munster Rd, SW6 6BT This Fulham-based bakery offers the most delicious sourdough bread.

Fabrique Bakery

Multiple locations, Holborn, Covent Garden, Fitzrovia If you can't decide between a cinnamon or cardamom bun, you should probably get both.

Miel Bakery

57 Warren St, W1T 5NR Everything here is delicious. Their sourdough is so good, and I somehow always end up with a chocolate chip cookie and passionfruit macaroon.

Aux Merveilleux de Fred

88 Old Brompton Rd, SW7 3LQ Go for the chocolate brioche, stay for the delicious meringues.

Comptoir Gourmand

Multiple locations, Soho, Bermondsey, Maltby Street, Borough French patisserie offering up classic bakes and irresistible treats.

Fortitude Bakehouse

35 Colonnade, WC1N 1JA Sourdough cakes, buns and loaves are on offer at this charming bakery.

Luminary Bakey

47 Chalk Farm Rd, NW1 8AJ The cinnamon rolls are divine.

Margot Bakery

121 E End Rd, N2 0SZ Sourdough is queen here and it is used in all the bakes.

Pophams Bakery

Multiple locations, Islington and Hackney The lamination of the dough here is incredible, and everything is delicious.

Söderberg Bakery

36 Berwick St, W1F 8RR If you are looking for a little fika, this is
the perfect place to get cinnamon buns.

The Old Post Office Bakery

76 Landor Rd, SW9 9PH An organic bakery offering up a
variety of delicious breads and treats.

Flor

Voyager Estate South 6, Spa Rd, SE16 4RP A must visit if you
are at Spa Terminus. Everything is divine.

Little Bread Pedlar

Spa Terminus, Dockley Rd, SE16 3FJ It is worth a trip to Spa
Terminus Market just to buy their bread.

Pavillion

18 Broadway Market, E8 4QJ Delicious bread. Delicious pizza.
What more could you want?

E5 Bakehouse

396 Mentmore Terrace, E8 3PH Bread, brownies, babka, brioche . . .
they do it all and it is all delicious.

The Dusty Knuckle

Abbot St, E8 3DP Serious sandwiches on incredible bread.

Jolene

21 Newington Green, N16 9PU On-site milled flour produces
the most delicious baked goods.

Bread Ahead

Borough Market, Cathedral Street, SE1 9DE Known for their filled
doughnuts and delicious pastries

LONDON

BY LOCALS

PART TWO

CHELSEA + CLAPHAM + REGENT'S CANAL + GREENWICH + HAMPSTEAD + ISLINGTON + MARYLEBONE + MAYFAIR + NOTTING HILL + RICHMOND + SHOREDITCH + SOUTH BANK

Victoria and Albert Museum

Harrods

Moyses Stevens

Bywater Street

MAÎTRE CHOUX

Bread Ahead

Maître Choux

Aux Merveilleux de Fred

Saatchi Gallery

Anthropologie

The Ivy Chelsea Garden

Manolo Blahnik

Royal Chelsea Hospital

Peggy Porschen

Chelsea Physic Garden

CHELSEA

Chelsea is full of history, having been home to the likes of Bram Stoker, P. L. Travers, Gertrude Bell, George Eliot, Alexander Fleming, Rosalind Franklin, A. A. Milne, Sylvia Pankhurst and Oscar Wilde. Its *vibrant past* can be felt today with top-tier shopping, world-class museums, art galleries, amazing restaurants and charming cafes - not to mention the always inspiring *Chelsea Flower Show* and accompanying Chelsea in Bloom, which annually brings multitudes of tourists to view the stunning floral displays that fill up the neighbourhood. From Sloane Square to Pavilion Road, and Bywater Street to Chelsea Embankment, there are *countless shops* and streets to explore.

So whether you are looking to do some shopping, check out a museum or gallery, eat a *delicious* meal or just wander through a beautiful neighbourhood, Chelsea is worth a visit.

Victoria and Albert Museum

Cromwell Rd, SW7 2RL Stunning museum with a beautiful cafe and a great mixture of collections. Don't miss the Cast Courts and the Raphael Cartoons.

Aux Merveilleux de Fred

88 Old Brompton Rd, SW7 3LQ Famed for their chocolate brioche and cloud-like merveilleuxs. My advice is to get two chocolate brioches, one for now and one for later, and a box of mini merveilleux.

Maître Choux

15 Harrington Rd, South Kensington, SW7 3ES Delicious and beautiful eclairs in every colour of the rainbow.

Harrods

87–135 Brompton Rd, SW1X 7XL I get lost every single time I go! I can never find the Egyptian escalators, and the food hall can get really busy, but it is a beautiful building with a veritable variety of treasures.

Bread Ahead

249 Pavilion Rd, SW1X 0BP Pavilion Road is full of delicious restaurants and charming shops. Pop into Bread Ahead for a loaf of their amazing sourdough and a few doughnuts just for good measure.

Moyses Stevens

188 Pavilion Rd, SW3 2BF Treat yourself to beautiful flowers at this royal warrant-holding florist.

Saatchi Gallery

Duke of York Square, SW3 4RY An amazing contemporary art gallery with ever-changing exhibits.

Royal Chelsea Hospital

Royal Hospital Rd, SW3 4SR You can tour this hospital year round, but once a year it is transformed for the Chelsea Flower Show. Something to be experienced at least once in life.

Chelsea Physic Garden

66 Royal Hospital Rd, SW3 4HS This garden started as an apothecaries' garden in 1673, growing plants for healing and medicine. Nowadays, the tradition lives on with medical plants still being grown there.

Anthropologie

131–141 King's Rd, SW3 4PW If you are looking for eclectic and fun homeware and clothing, this is the store for you. Marvel at the beautiful building that houses it as well.

The Ivy Chelsea Garden

195–197 King's Rd, SW3 5EQ Seasonally decorated outside and good food inside. This is the perfect place to go for dinner with friends.

Peggy Porschen

219 King's Rd, SW3 5EJ The second cafe of this darling and delicious cake shop offers a full range of breakfasts and lunches as well as treats.

Bywater Street

SW3 4TR There are many colourful streets in Chelsea, but this is one of my favourites.

Manolo Blahnik

49–51 Old Church St, SW3 5BS
Visit the first Manolo shop and daydream about where you would wear the fabulous shoes.

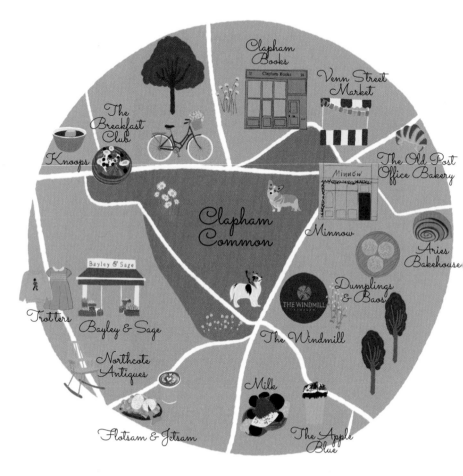

Clapham Books

Venn Street Market

The Breakfast Club

Knoops

The Old Post Office Bakery

Minnow

Clapham Common

Aries Bakehouse

Bayley & Sage

Trotters

Dumplings & Baos

Bayley & Sage

THE WINDMILL

The Windmill

Northcote Antiques

Milk

Flotsam & Jetsam

The Apple Blue

CLAPHAM

I love how each corner of London has its own unique vibe, its own independent shops, restaurants, bakeries and coffee shops that locals don't want anyone else to know about. Clapham is a *charming area* just south of the river Thames. With Clapham Common at its core, the surrounding streets are full of restaurants, shops, pubs and bakeries. This area is popular with *families and young adults* alike, with lots of lively clubs as well as family-friendly restaurants. It is a great place to *explore*, especially on a Saturday, when you can visit Venn Street Market.

Aries Bakehouse

99 Acre Ln, SW2 5TU Serving up cruffins, sourdough
and pastries of all sorts.

Bayley & Sage

95 Northcote Rd, SW11 6PL Upmarket grocery store with an amazing
selection of seasonal produce, cheeses and artisanal foods.

Clapham Books

26 The Pavement, SW4 0JA Local independent bookshop with a great
selection of books. You're bound to leave with something great.

Dumplings & Baos

31 Clapham Park Rd, SW4 7EE Fluffy and delicious steamed
buns, tasty dumplings and classic Chinese dishes are served here.

Flotsam & Jetsam

4 Bellevue Parade, SW17 7EQ Serving up delicious food,
great drinks and a lovely atmosphere.

Knoops

64 St John's Rd, SW11 1PS Artisanal hot chocolate with
an extensive range of chocolates to choose from.

Milk

18–20 Bedford Hill, SW12 9RG Great coffee and delicious food. Their
buckwheat pancakes are the perfect weekend indulgence.

Minnow

21 The Pavement, SW4 0HY Looking over Clapham Common
and serving up great food from breakfast to dinner.

Northcote Antiques Market

155A Northcote Rd, SW11 6QB A treasure trove of antiques selling everything from furniture to artwork.

The Apple Blue

212 Balham High Rd, SW12 9BS A great brunch spot offering mouthwatering mains and great drinks.

Venn Street Market

Venn St, SW4 0AT Saturday market selling delicious food and crafts.

The Old Post Office Bakery

76 Landor Rd, SW9 9PH Organic breads and pastries hand-crafted daily.

The Windmill

Clapham Common South Side, SW4 9DE Hotel and pub with a great garden, classic pub fare and cool atmosphere.

Trotters

86 Northcote Rd, SW11 6QN Classic British children's clothing brand selling timeless pieces and iconic styles.

The Breakfast Club

5–9 Battersea Rise, SW11 1HG American diner-style restaurant serving up pancakes, burgers and English breakfasts.

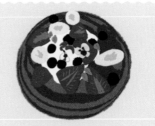

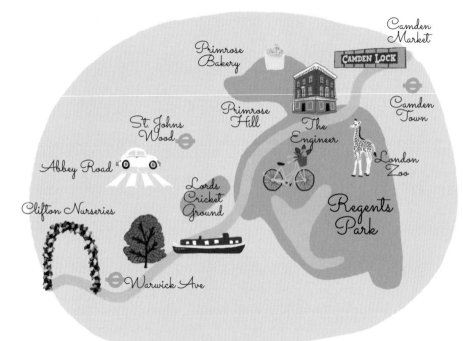

Camden
Market

Primrose
Bakery

CAMDEN LOCK

Camden
Town

Primrose
Hill

St. Johns
Wood

The
Engineer

London
Zoo

Abbey Road

Regents
Park

Lords
Cricket
Ground

Clifton Nurseries

Warwick Ave

REGENT'S CANAL

A walk along Regent's Canal is a wonderful weekend activity. The canal path offers *lovely views* of boats and houses as you wind your way from start to finish. The walk is just over two miles and is very *family friendly*. The path is fully paved and you can easily take your bike or a pram. There are so many delicious restaurants and cafes at either end of the walk that no matter where you start and finish you can always get something delicious to eat! When you are walking through Regent's Park, be sure to *admire the manor houses* with the beautifully manicured gardens, and as you get closer to London Zoo keep an eye out for birds and animals. You can sense when you are getting closer to Camden as the *vibe changes*. You will see artists selling their art, musicians busking and murals and graffiti adorning the walls.

The Engineer

65 Gloucester Ave, NW1 8JD
This is a charming gastro pub located just off Regent's Canal. The food is excellent and the atmosphere is great.

Warwick Ave

W9 2PT Also known as Little Venice, due to the nature of the canals, this is a lovely corner of London. Check out Formosa Street, which is home to The Brimful Store and Formosa Flowers Chocolaterie, as well as the pub The Prince Alfred.

Clifton Nurseries

5A Clifton Villas, W9 2PH This garden centre/cafe is a truly hidden gem. Tucked between two houses, it is very easy to walk right past the entrance. Once you've found it, the garden path leads you to a plant oasis and charming cafe, which serves breakfast, brunch, lunch and afternoon tea.

Primrose Hill

Primrose Hill Rd, NW1 4NR You can turn off the canal path into Primrose Hill. Here you'll find charming pubs, restaurants and colourful houses. Even though it is only a few minutes away from Camden, it feels like a world apart.

Primrose Bakery

69 Gloucester Ave, NW1 8LD Take your cupcake to go and sit in Chalcot Square. Every house around the garden is painted a different colour and they are all amazing. You could even sit in the garden and enjoy the rainbow houses while potentially eating a rainbow cupcake!

Camden Market

Camden Lock Pl, NW1 8AF

The canal path leads right into Camden Lock, which is the home the famous Camden Market, a foodie mecca selling every type of food that you can imagine. Camden Market is a very popular tourist destination so it is often quite crowded.

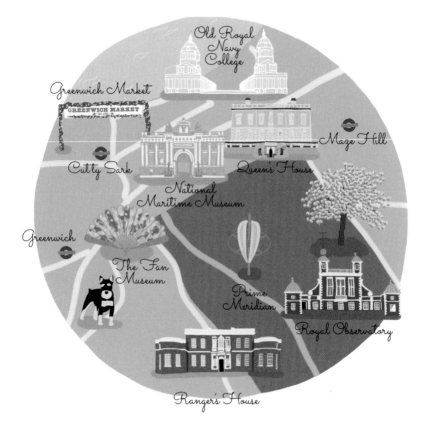

Old Royal Navy College

Greenwich Market

GREENWICH MARKET

Maze Hill

Cutty Sark

Queens House

National Maritime Museum

Greenwich

The Fan Museum

Prime Meridian

Royal Observatory

Ranger's House

GREENWICH

Greenwich is a delightful village in London that feels like it's a world away. With *quaint streets*, charming shops, stunning architecture and sweeping views, this World Heritage Site is a *lovely place* to spend a day.

There have been settlements here since the Bronze Age, making it ripe with history. King Henry VIII, Queen Elizabeth I and Queen Mary I were all born at the *Palace of Placentia*, which used to stand where the Old Royal Navy College now is. Today you can still enjoy the *Palladian* architecture designed by Christopher Wren and Inigo Jones, as well as tour *The Royal Observatory* where scientists develop methods to calculate longitude and create *Greenwich Mean Time* – the standard against which all other time zones are based.

Prime Meridian

Blackheath Ave, SE10 8XJ
Located within the observatory is the Prime
Meridian, where longitude, a man-made
designation used by all to measure your
location on the earth vertically, is 0°.

Royal Observatory

Blackheath Ave, SE10 8XJ Designed by Christopher Wren and
the scientist Robert Hooke, observations made here cemented
it as the home of time and longitude. Stargaze in the middle of the day
with a planetarium show.

Queen's House

Romney Rd, SE10 9NF The Queen's House, designed by Inigo Jones, was
the first Palladian building in England.

National Maritime Museum

Romney Rd, SE10 9NF A wonderful museum with an extensive collection
focused on maritime and navigational history.

Greenwich Market

London SE10 9HZ A lovely market with delicious food and local artisans
selling their wares. The perfect place to pick up some lunch for a picnic
in the park.

The Fan Museum

12 Crooms Hill, SE10 8ER A quirky museum dedicated to the history and making of fans. They also have a charming orangerie serving tea and cakes.

Ranger's House

Chesterfield Walk, SE10 8QX An English Heritage site housing a beautiful art collection, including a Botticelli.

Old Royal Navy College

King William Walk, SE10 9NN
The building, designed by Christopher Wren, is an architectural masterpiece in and of itself, but inside you simply cannot miss the epically baroque Painted Hall.

Kenwood House

Golders Hill
Park

D.H.
LAWRENCE
1885–1930
Novelist and Poet
lived here
1915

Hampstead
Heath

Bathing
Ponds

The Holly
Bush

JOHN
GALSWORTHY
1867–1933
NOVELIST AND
PLAYWRIGHT
lived here
1918–1933

DAPHNE DU MAURIER
1907–1989
NOVELIST
LIVED HERE
1917–1934

Fenton House

Oddono's

Le Creperie de
Hampstead

Roni's

Daunt
Books

The
Nook

HAMPSTEAD

Hampstead is one of my favourite places in London. It feels miles away from the hustle and bustle and is popular with locals and tourists alike. It is full of *lovely restaurants* and shops and has a vibrant *literary* history. Walking the winding streets and charming alleys of Hampstead Village feels like you are exploring a *beautiful maze* and you get rewarded with the cutest houses and *stunning views*. As you wander further from the high street and onto the Heath, London fades into the background and you can enjoy the *rambling tree-lined paths* and wide meadows.

Hampstead Bathing Ponds

Hampstead Heath, NW5 1QR
There are three bathing ponds on the Heath: a women's pond, a men's pond and a mixed pond. Enjoy a dip year round if you can bear it, but the ponds are most crowded in the warmer months.

Fenton House

Fenton House, Hampstead Grove, NW3 6SP A National Trust property that has the most charming apple orchard from which they produce their own delicious apple juice.

Kenwood House

Hampstead Ln, NW3 7JR Nestled into the northern-most part of Hampstead Heath, Kenwood House is a stunning home that is free to visit. It has a vibrant history and the cutest pastel library.

Le Creperie de Hampstead

77 Hampstead High St, NW3 1RE This little crêpe stand almost always has a line, but it is always worth the wait. They make the most delicious crêpes with both savoury and sweet fillings. You can't go wrong with your order here, as everything is delicious.

Oddono's

8 Flask Walk, NW3 1HE The perfect place to stop for yummy gelato on a warm summer's day, or a cool winter's day, or any day. Their gelato is delicious year round.

The Hill Garden and Pergola

The Pergola, Inverforth Cl, NW3 7EX Located right next to the Heath is Golders Hill Park, a charming and often less crowded park. It boasts a small menagerie as well as a deer enclosure. However, my favouite part is the Hill Garden and Pergola, which feels like a secret enchanted garden.

Roni's

44 Rosslyn Hill, NW3 1NH One of the best places to get New York-style bagels in London. Pop into the cafe for a tasty brunch, or just grab a bag of bagels to enjoy throughout the week.

Daunt Books

51 S End Rd, NW3 2QB A quaint bookshop to browse through, with an exceptional selection of books. The perfect place to find your next great read.

The Nook

43 S End Rd, NW3 2PY A charming little cafe and a great place to stop and refuel before or after a walk on the Heath. Enjoy a hot cocoa in the cooler months or, once the weather is warmer, ice cream or a milkshake.

The Holly Bush

22 Holly Mount, NW3 6SG

Tucked away on a dead-end street, The Holly Bush is one of the cosiest and most charming pubs around. Enjoy their Sunday roast with the fireplace crackling in the background.

Cookies and Scream

Urban Social

Paper Mâche Tiger

molly meg

Udderlicious

Untitled Flowers

Molly Meg

Aria

Sproot

Ottolenghi

Pophams

THE PIG BUTCHER PUB

ALMEIDA THEATRE

Almeida Theatre

The Pig and Butcher

Little Angel Theatre

Present & Correct

Sadler Wells Theatre

Victoria Miro Gallery

72

ISLINGTON

Upper Street in Islington is a lovely place to wander along.
The mile-long stretch from *Angel* up to Highbury and
Islington is full of shops, restaurants, bakeries, theatres
and *green spaces* to enjoy.

Explore the antique shops and cafes of Camden Passage, get
a scoop of ice cream from Udderlicious (one of the *best* ice
cream shops in London), enjoy the English National Ballet
at Sadler Wells or a show at the Almeida. For dinner options
you are spoilt for choice as there are seemingly *countless*
restaurants along the high road.

Udderlicious

187 Upper St, N1 1RQ
My absolute favourite ice cream in London.
If I am near one of their two locations I
always stop and get a scoop, no matter the
weather. My favourite flavour is the dark
chocolate sea salt sorbet.

Paper Mache Tiger

26 Cross St, N1 2BG This store is so cool. It is a cafe/clothing/homeware/
plant store. You won't regret a wander through.

Molly Meg

111 Essex Rd, N1 2SL One of my favourite children's clothing stores in
London. If you can't make it to Islington, check out their online store.

Aria Barnsbury Hall

2B Barnsbury St, N1 1PN A lovely homeware store with beautiful things
to fill your home.

Ottolenghi

287 Upper St, N1 2TZ One of my favourite restaurants in London. The
food is fresh and delicious and has the best flavours.

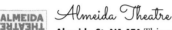

Almeida Theatre

Almeida St, N1 1TA This off-West-End theatre is one of my favourites.

Sproot

116D Upper St, N1 1QP Delicious plant-based cafe serving up tasty salads,
smoothies and coffee.

The Pig and Butcher

80 Liverpool Rd, N1 0QD A cosy gastro pub with delicious food. Be sure to save room for dessert!

Pophams

19 Prebend St, N1 8PF Unique flavours and delicious viennoiserie. Blood orange and dark chocolate custard pastry anyone?

Victoria Miro Gallery

16 Wharf Rd, N1 7RW Pop in to see whatever cool exhibition they have on.

Cookies and Scream

130 Holloway Rd, N7 8JE A vegan and gluten-free bakery offering brownies, cookies, milkshakes and more.

Little Angel Theatre

14 Dagmar Passage, N1 2DN A theatre that is just for kids. I especially love their puppet shows! They have shows for all ages, from babies to older kids.

Present & Correct

23 Arlington Way, EC1R 1UY One of the best stationery stores in London. With retro-inspired paper and office goods, you won't be able to leave empty handed.

Urban Social

236 Upper St, N1 1RU A great spot for smoothies, brunch or a cup of coffee.

Untitled Flowers

6 Shillingford St, N1 2DP
Beautiful flower shop with the loveliest arrangements.

The Conran Shop

Daunt Books

The Ginger Pig

Fishers

La Brasseria

Rococo Chocolates

La Fromagerie

Pierre Marcolini

Daylesford

V V Rouleaux

Chiltern Firehouse

The Monocle Cafe

The Wallace Collection

Paul Rothe & Son

MARYLEBONE

Found between Baker Street and Oxford Street, Marylebone High Street is centrally located but just enough off the beaten path that it is *not crowded* with tourists. The street is full of clothing stores, restaurants, speciality shops and one of London's *best bookshops*. Marylebone is one of my go-to areas to take visiting family and friends. The variety of restaurants and shops makes for a *lovely day out*. Just off the high street is one of my favourite museums as well.

The Wallace Collection is often passed over for some of the more famous museums in London, but I would *highly recommend* going. It is quite small but houses a brilliant collection of art, furniture, trinkets, weapons and armour, as well as the loveliest pink cafe.

Fishers

50 Marylebone High St, W1U 5HN If you are looking to eat schnitzels and sausages with the ambiance of 1920s Vienna, this is the place for you. The food is traditional Viennese and does not disappoint. Be sure to get a side of spätzle.

Pierre Marcolini

37 Marylebone High St, W1U 4QE Beautiful patisserie and chocolates created by the Belgian master chocolatier Pierre Marcolini. The desserts here are equally beautiful and delicious.

La Fromagerie

2–6 Moxon St, W1U 4EW This is what cheese heaven looks like. Seriously. They have the most amazing selection of cheese and a staff full of knowledge who are happy to help you find exactly what you need. They also serve breakfast and lunch.

Rococo Chocolates

3 Moxon St, W1U 4EP Delicious chocolate in interesting flavours with the smoothest finish. In the cooler months they have the thickest hot cocoa in amazing flavours. Try their Regent's Park honey truffles or pumpkin truffles.

Daylesford

6–8 Blandford St, W1U 4AU Cafe and organic farm shop with delicious produce and great food.

Paul Rothe & Son

35 Marylebone Ln, W1U 2NN Old-fashioned local deli serving up tasty soup and sandwiches. If you go at lunchtime, plan on joining a queue as it is a popular place for locals to grab a quick bite.

The Ginger Pig

8–10 Moxon St, W1U 4EW A great selection of high-quality meats are on offer at this butcher, as well as delicious sausage rolls. They also offer butchery classes.

La Brasseria

42 Marylebone High St, W1U 5HD On a warm day this is the perfect place to sit outside and people watch as you enjoy your meal. Serving Italian classics as well breakfast staples.

The Monocle Café

18 Chiltern St, W1U 7QA Charming cafe with a great selection of pastries and drinks. Snag a table if you can and enjoy the view onto idyllic Chiltern Street.

Chiltern Firehouse

1 Chiltern St, W1U 7PA This former firehouse has found a new life as a high-end hotel and restaurant. It is the perfect place for a special occasion or weekend breakfast.

The Wallace Collection

Hertford House, Manchester Square, W1U 3BN Peyton and Byrne operate this pink cafe within the Wallace Collection. The food is good and the ambiance is amazing. This is one of my go-to places to take friends who are visiting London. We stop here for lunch or dessert after exploring the area and the museum.

The Conran Shop

55 Marylebone High St, W1U 5HS The Conran Shop is probably my favourite shop in London, up there with Liberty of London. They have the coolest home accessories and furniture, and walking through the store is simply a pleasure.

Daunt Books

84 Marylebone High St, W1U 4QW One of London's best bookstores. The staff are knowledgeable and the selection of books incredible.

V V Rouleaux

102 Marylebone Ln, W1U 2QD A modern haberdashery full of the most dreamy ribbons, pom poms, braids, feathers and much, much more.

Mercato

Claridge's
Hotel

Sketch London

Royal Academy of Arts

NAC

The Royal Institute

Fortnum & Maso

The Connaught
Patisserie

Burlington Arcade

Kitty Fishers

The Ritz

Shepherd Market

SHEPHERD
MARKET W1
CITY OF WESTMINSTER

The Wolseley

Le Deli
Robuchon

MAYFAIR

Mayfair is one of London's most high-end and historic areas. Pocketed between Green Park and Bond Street, it has been *popular* since the first homes were built here in the 1700s. A walk through Mayfair feels like a walk through what London would have been like *hundreds of years* ago.

Now it is home to luxury hotels, Michelin-starred restaurants, top-end shops and world-famous galleries, the *beautiful architecture* of the area hasn't changed much since the 1800s.

While many of the shops are in the luxury price range, there are lovely places to stop for a meal that won't set you back too much. Regardless of whether you are window shopping or looking to spend big, *strolling* through Mayfair is a delight.

Mercato

Mayfair St. Mark's Church, North Audley St, W1K 6ZA
This Grade I-listed church has been repurposed into a stunning food hall. With traders cooking up food from across the globe, you are sure to find something delicious.

NAC

41 North Audley St, W1K 6ZP A charming restaurant with delicious food served morning to night. A great place to rest and refuel after exploring the area.

The Connaught Patisserie

The Connaught, Carlos Pl, W1K 2AL While a stay at The Connaught might be above most budgets, a stop by The Connaught Patisserie is a worthy splurge. This beautifully designed patisserie sells a delicious range of decadent desserts and drinks.

Kitty Fishers

10 Shepherd Market, W1J 7QF A local favourite with great food and amazing atmosphere, all housed in a charming location.

Le Deli Robuchon

82 Piccadilly, W1J 8JA An amazing deli offering up all you need to fill your picnic basket. A great place to stop to pick up some lunch or treats to enjoy on a sunny day in Green Park.

Shepherd Market

London W1J 7QU A delightful pocket of Mayfair with restaurants and boutique shops.

The Ritz

150 Piccadilly, St James's, W1J 9BR This iconic London hotel has been a landmark since it opened in the early 1900s. It is a great place to go for one of the most classic afternoon teas.

The Wolseley

160 Piccadilly, St James's, W1J 9EB Stop in at any time of the day for excellent food in this beautiful art deco restaurant.

Fortnum & Mason

181 Piccadilly, St James's, W1A 1ER A London icon since 1707 offering up afternoon tea, ice cream at the parlour and a grocery store full of the finest foods.

Burlington Arcade

51 Piccadilly, W1J 0QJ This shopping arcade is full of luxury shops. Don't miss the gilded Ladurée selling macrons in every flavour in a golden cave.

The Royal Institute

21 Albemarle St, W1S 4BS Home to the Faraday Museum, the Royal Institute also organises workshops and lectures for children and adults.

Royal Academy of Arts

Burlington House, Piccadilly, W1J 0BD Rotating exhibitions throughout the year with the Summer Exhibition at the top of the art social calendar.

Claridge's Hotel

Brook Street, W1K 4HR If you are looking for a Michelin-star restaurant or an amazing afternoon tea, you won't be disappointed.

Sketch London

9 Conduit St, W1S 2XG
One of the most memorable places to enjoy afternoon tea in London.

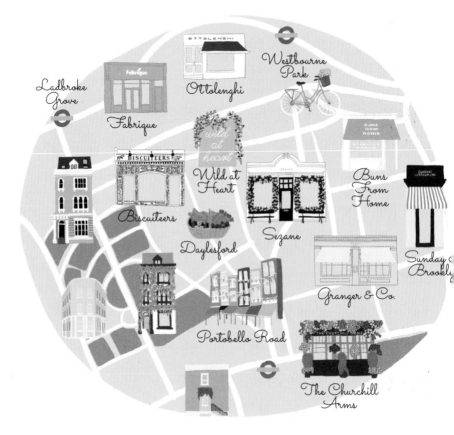

Ladbroke Grove

Fabrique

Ottolenghi

Westbourne Park

Wild at Heart

Biscuiteers

Daylesford

Sezane

Buns From Home

Sunday Brooklyn

Granger & Co.

Portobello Road

The Churchill Arms

NOTTING HILL

Notting Hill is one of London's most iconic neighbourhoods. Dotted with *colourful streets*, delicious cafes, restaurants and bakeries, as well as all sorts of shops from antique to boutique, it is no wonder it is so *popular*.

There is a lot to *explore* in this relatively small area. If you are looking to walk down streets of rainbow-coloured houses, head to Farmer Street or Elgin Crescent. If you are wanting to visit the weekend market, head to *Portobello Road*. And if you are up for some shopping or a *lovely meal*, Westbourne Grove is the place for you.

The Churchill Arms

119 Kensington Church St, W8 7LN

One of the most photogenic pubs in London serving up Thai food and refreshing drinks.

Portobello Road

W10 5TY

At the weekend the full market comes to life, but all the shops along the road are open during the week. Perfect if you are on the hunt for antiques, vintage finds and collectables.

Buns From Home

128 Talbot Rd, W11 1JA Delicious buns and focaccia, with weekend specials that always sell out.

Granger & Co.

175 Westbourne Grove, W11 2SB A classic breakfast spot that is popular with locals and tourists alike. If you like pancakes, try their ricotta hotcakes.

Sunday In Brooklyn

98 Westbourne Grove, W2 5RU The London outpost of this Brooklyn eatery. Everything here is so good. My favourites are the pancakes with hazelnut maple praline and the cauliflower patty melt.

Daylesford

208–212 Westbourne Grove, W11 2RH A lovely farm shop/cafe/homeware store. A great place to stop for lunch or a bit of shopping.

Ottolenghi

63 Ledbury Rd, W11 2AD A great spot to pick up some takeaway for a picnic in the park or to enjoy at home. Everything is so good here. From the baked treats to the fresh salads, you really can't go wrong.

Fabrique

212 Portobello Rd, W11 1LA This is THE place to go for traditional Scandi cinnamon or cardamom buns.

Biscuiteers

194 Kensington Park Rd, W11 2ES Delightful biscuits beautifully iced. They also do a charming afternoon tea, as well as hosting icing classes so you can learn how to create your own edible masterpiece.

Wild at Heart

222 Westbourne Grove, W11 2RH The flowers here don't come cheap, but the building is a work of art, and the floral displays are always stunning.

Westbourne Grove

W11 2R

This colourful street lined with restaurants and shops is a lively area to explore. There are charming children's boutiques such as Mini Rodini, La Coqueta, Bon Point, Bon Ton and Carmel. For adults don't miss Sezane or Toast.

Orleans House Gallery

Marble Hill House

Richmond Bridge

Richmond Hill

Petersham Nurseries

Richmond Park

Ham House

RICHMOND

Richmond is a charming village within London. It is full of restaurants, cafes and an *abundance of green space*, and it is home to one of London's most *lovely* river walks. The Richmond Thames Path offers scenic views and leads you to *dreamy destinations* with great food and drink options dotted along the way. As you stroll along the *Thames* you will see rowers glide along the water, families enjoying a picnic in the park, *cyclists out for a long ride* and friends enjoying a leisurely walk. The walk along the south side of the Thames will take you to Ham House, a *National Trust* site that is well worth a visit if you enjoy visiting stately homes. The north side of the Thames offers Marble Hill House and Orleans House Gallery as great destinations.

With *ample greenery* from spring to summer, this is a great walk to enjoy on a warm weekend, but is lovely year round.

Ham House

Ham St, Ham, Richmond TW10 7RS A National Trust property with lovely interiors and classic gardens. During wisteria season the garden cafe is covered in purple blooms and is a lovely spot to stop and enjoy some tea. If you are looking for a fun way to cross the river, Hammerton's Ferry takes you across the Thames to Marble Hill House for just £1.

Richmond Bridge

Richmond TW9 1EW Built in 1776, this iconic bridge is a local landmark. You can rent a rowboat at the base of the bridge and paddle around, or enjoy a drink at one of the cafes in the gardens next to the bridge.

Richmond Hill

Richmond Hill, Richmond TW10 A beautiful view of the Thames with a telescope to spot things below.

Marble Hill House

Richmond Rd, Twickenham TW1 2NL An English Heritage site, this 18th-century Palladian-style villa was built for Henrietta Howard, mistress of King George II. Freshly refurbished, it is free to visit.

Orleans House Gallery

Orleans Rd, Twickenham TW1 3BL A contemporary art gallery housed in a Palladian-style mansion. It runs a range of kid-friendly activities and has woodlands and a playground near the Thames.

Petersham Nurseries

Church Lane, Petersham Rd, TW10 7AB
Enjoy a relaxing tea at the tea house, a lovely meal at their cafe or get garden inspiration in this enchanting botanical setting.

A New Tribe

Hackney City Farm

Aida Shoreditch

Columbia Road Flower Market

Lyle's Tea Building

Dark Sugars

Brick Lane Bookshop

166 Brick Lane Bookshop 166

BEIGEL BAKE
BRICK LANE BAKERY
OPEN 24 HOURS 7 DAYS

Beigel Bake

TRUMAN

Bricklane Bookshop

Soft Serve Society

Rinkoff Bakery

Padella Pasta

Truman Brewery

Libreria

Burro e Salvia

LIVERPOOL STREET

Libreria Bookshop

Dennis Severs' House

Spitalfields Market

SHOREDITCH

One of the most diverse areas in London, Shoreditch is *steeped in history*. Shakespeare's plays were performed in Elizabethan times at a theatre in Shoreditch, which was located just outside the *City of London*; French Huguenots brought their silk-weaving skills to the area as they fled persecution in France in the 1600s; and the Victorian Spitalfields market *still* stands today.

This area was heavily bombed during WWII and has since been rebuilt, gentrified and *redeveloped* into the very hip neighbourhood it is today. This area is known for its food scene, *amazing markets*, independent shops, world-class graffiti and historic buildings. There is simply *no other place* in London quite like it. With a grunge vibe, artistic attitude and devil-may-care mood, exploring Shoreditch is a great way to spend a day.

A New Tribe

273 Hackney Rd, E2 8NA Beautifully curated homewares with a stunning selection of Moroccan rugs.

Aida Shoreditch

133 Shoreditch High St, E1 6JE Homeware as well as men's and women's wear, with a focus on style and sustainability.

Hackney City Farm

1a Goldsmiths Row, E2 8QA A charming farm in the middle of the city. A perfect place to take your little ones.

Columbia Road Flower Market

Columbia Rd, E2 7RG A plant-lovers paradise pops up on Columbia Road every Sunday. There are also dozens of little homewares shops and cute cafes to stop by.

Lyle's Tea Building

56 Shoreditch High St, E1 6JJ Modern British restaurant with a focus on quality local and seasonal ingredients. You can taste the passion in the food here.

Beigel Bake

159 Brick Ln, E1 6SB This London icon is open 24 hours and serves up bagels with delicious fillings such as salt beef, cream cheese, Nutella and more.

Dark Sugars

141 Brick Lane, E1 6SB A must visit for any chocolate lover. Definitely try their hot chocolate.

Bricklane Bookshop

166 Brick Lane, E1 6RU A lovely independent bookshop with a great selection of local books.

Burro e Salvia

52 Redchurch St, E2 7DP Fresh pasta and provisions that you can take away or enjoy in their cafe.

Rinkoff Bakery

79 Vallance Rd, E1 5BS Crodoughs, challa and colourful bagels grace the counter at this 100-year-old bakery.

Truman Brewery

91 Brick Ln, E1 6QR There are a lot of different markets that pop up on Brick Lane, but two that are especially great are The Sunday Upmarket and the Backyard Market.

Padella Pasta

1 Phipp St, EC2A 4PS Handmade pasta that will make you feel like you are in Italy.

Dennis Severs' House

18 Folgate St, E1 6BX London has no shortage of interesting museums, but this is like none other. As you wander through the rooms in this immersive museum you are transported to what life would have been like from the 1700s to the 1900s.

Spitalfields Market

56 Brushfield St, E1 6AA One of London's oldest markets selling art, clothing, homewares and food. Some favourite places to eat are Crosstown Doughnuts, Dumpling Shack, Humble Crumble, Yum Bun and Bleecker Burger.

Libreria Bookshop

65 Hanbury St, E1 5JP A truly enchanting bookshop that is designed to help you discover new books you might have missed otherwise.

Soft Serve Society

Multiple locations, Victoria, Shoreditch, Covent Garden Soft serve ice cream and milkshakes with amazing topping options.

Somerset House

St Paul's Cathedral

Tower of London

Big Ben

Cleopatra's Needle

National Theatre

Tower Bridge

Westminster Abbey

Tate Modern

Globe Theatre

BOROUGH MARKET

London Eye

Borough Market

SOUTH BANK

If you want a walk that really packs in a lot then *I highly recommend* a stroll along the South Bank of the Thames. This is my go-to walk when I have friends or family visiting. It takes you past a *majority* of big sites and gives you stunning views of the city. There is also lots of good food to eat along the way, so plan on stopping to grab a bite *or a pint* and soak in the atmosphere.

I wouldn't recommend trying to visit everything along this route in one day as that would be too exhausting. Pick out a few things you want to do, then enjoy the scenery of the other *landmarks* as you pass by. There is thousands of years of history along the Thames and something for everyone to enjoy – whether you're a *medievalist* or a modern art lover.

Tower of London

EC3N 4AB
Perfect for people who love
the history of England and
the Crown Jewels.

Tower Bridge

Tower Bridge Rd, SE1 2UP You can see this iconic bridge at many places
along the South Bank. You can also climb to the top and walk across its
glass floor as you enjoy sweeping views of London.

Borough Market

8 Southwark St, SE1 1TL One of London's oldest markets. There are
so many delicious food options here, you can't go wrong.

Tate Modern

Bankside, SE1 9TG If you love modern art this is a great museum
to explore. They have kids' trails as well so it can be really fun for
little ones.

National Theatre

Upper Ground, SE1 9PX If you are a theatre lover, seeing a show here is a
great way to spend the evening. They also have a wonderful bookshop that
is worth wandering through.

London Eye

Riverside Building, SE1 7PB If the weather is good you can get amazing
views of London from here.

Westminster Abbey

20 Deans Yd, SW1P 3PA There is so much history here. It is one of the few places I think everyone who visits or lives in London should go to.

Big Ben

SW1A 0AA It's fun to walk by this icon. For a great photo spot, cross Westminster Bridge and view the Houses of Parliament from the south side of the Thames.

Cleopatra's Needle

WC2N 6PB This 3,500-year-old obelisk was gifted to the UK in the early 1800s as a thank you for help in military campaigns. It sailed to London from Egypt, and almost sank during the journey, but now has been proudly standing in this spot since 1878.

Somerset House

Strand, WC2R 1LA Art galleries, cafes and restaurants all in a beautiful setting. The Courtauld Gallery has an amazing collection of art; Watch House is a great place to stop for a coffee or tea; and if you are looking for a nice meal, dine at Spring.

St Paul's Cathedral

St. Paul's Churchyard, EC4M 8AD An imposing cathedral and masterpiece designed by Sir Christopher Wren after the Great Fire.

Globe Theatre

21 New Globe Walk, SE1 9DT
If you are a Shakespeare fan then enjoying a show here is a real treat. If you can take or leave a show, then walking past it is good enough.

LONDON

BY INTEREST

PART THREE

ROYAL LONDON + MUSEUMS + PALACES + COLOURFUL LONDON
+ CYCLING LONDON + SCIENTIFIC LONDON + BOOKSHOPS
+ LONDON WITH KIDS + SUFFRAGETTE LONDON + LITERARY LONDON

Lock & Co
Hatters

Prestat Chocolates

Fortnum &
Mason

Hatchards Booksellers

The Tower of London

Paxton &
Whitfield

St Paul's
Cathedral

Kensington
Palace

Buckingham
Palace

Tower Bridge

The
Royal
Mews

Westminster
Abbey

The Queen's House

Hampton Court Palace

ROYAL LONDON

When it comes to Royal London, there is more to explore
than just palaces and castles. From the well-known
palaces to churches with *special places* in history
and shops holding royal warrants, this map brings
you the *royal best.*
With over 950 years of *history* across this map,
it covers everything from monarchs of old to where
Queen Elizabeth II buys her chocolates.
And a quick history lesson: *royal warrants* are
granted to places that supply goods or services to
the Queen, King or Prince of Wales.

The Tower of London

EC3N 4AB (Built 1066) Home to the Crown Jewels and the legendary Yeomen Warders. Nothing takes you back in time like a visit to the Tower.

Westminster Abbey

20 Deans Yd, SW1P 3PA (Built 1090) The headquarters for the Church of England, it has held coronations, royal weddings and funerals. Famous kings, queens, statesmen, soldiers, poets and scientists now rest beneath its hallowed halls.

Hampton Court Palace

Hampton Ct Way, Molesey, KT8 9AU (Built 1514) The main residence of King Henry VIII and his infamous wives. The gardens here are divine and home to beautiful woodland creatures like deer and swans.

Kensington Palace

Kensington Gardens, W8 4PX (Built 1605) The childhood home of Queen Victoria, where her elegant statue now sits out front. It is also the current residence of Prince William and his family.

The Queen's House

Romney Rd, Greater, SE10 9NF (Built 1616) The first classical building in the UK and currently home to many great works of art. The Tulip Stairs are a must-see.

St Paul's Cathedral

St Paul's Churchyard, EC4M 8AD (Built 1675) One of the most iconic landmarks in London, it is often featured in Hollywood films, like *Mary Poppins*. Royal weddings and state funerals are also held here. Climbing to the top of the central dome is one of my favourite things to do in London.

Buckingham Palace

SW1A 1AA (Built 1703) Headquarters and an official royal residence of the monarch, it is one of the most iconic buildings in London. If you go to London in the summer then the State Rooms are a must-see.

The Royal Mews

Buckingham Palace Rd, SW1W 0QH (Built 1825) Home to royal carriages from monarchs past and present, plus one of the finest displays of horses. The Queen's Diamond Jubilee State Coach is a personal favourite.

Tower Bridge

Tower Bridge Rd, SE1 2UP (Built 1886) One of the better kept secrets of London is that you can actually climb inside Tower Bridge. It's of my favourite things to do in the city, especially at sunset. There's even a glass floor to see down to the River Thames below!

Paxton & Whitfield

93 Jermyn St, SW1Y 6JE (Royal warrant 1850) Britain's leading cheesemonger. Queen Victoria became the first of many royals to name them as official royal cheesemonger. Their royal warrant means the King or Queen have first call on the best cheese in the land.

Hatchards Booksellers

187 Piccadilly, St. James's, W1J 9LE (Royal warrant 1901) This is London's oldest bookshop and Queen Charlotte was one of their first customers. The bookseller currently holds three royal warrants.

Fortnum & Mason

181 Piccadilly, St James's, W1A 1ER (Royal warrant 1955) They hold two royal warrants, making them the official tea merchants and grocers to HRH Queen Elizabeth II.

Lock & Co Hatters

6 St James's St, St James's, SW1A 1EF (Royal warrant 1956) The world's oldest hat shop and the oldest family-owned business in existence. Sir Winston Churchill even donned one of these hats making it his signature look.

Prestat Chocolates

14 Princes Arcade, SW1Y 6DS (Royal warrant 1975) I whole-heartedly agree with HRH Queen Elizabeth II on her choice of Royal Purveyor of Chocolates. A box of Prestat is the best gift anyone can ask for.

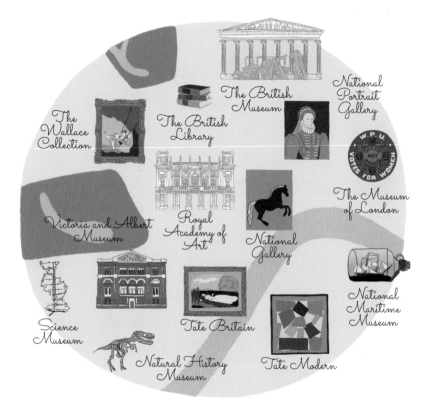

The British Museum

National Portrait Gallery

The Wallace Collection

The British Library

Victoria and Albert Museum

Royal Academy of Art

The Museum of London

National Gallery

Science Museum

Tate Britain

National Maritime Museum

Natural History Museum

Tate Modern

MUSEUMS

A visit to a museum can be a wonderful thing, and London has some of the *most visited* museums in the world. They are almost all free to visit, making them *popular with locals* and tourists alike. There are *world-class* collections ranging from million-year-old fossils and mummies to modern inventions such as the computer. These museums are great places to *discover* the history of the world, see priceless works of art and learn about world cultures.

These museums are *extensive* in both size and the scale of their collections, so it is worth doing a bit of research and prioritising what you would like to see. If you love *impressionist art* then don't miss the National Gallery; if you are fascinated by science then the Science and Natural History Museums are a must. And for the modern art lover, the Tate Modern is the place to go.

National Gallery

Trafalgar Square, WC2N 5DN Housing paintings from all the greats, from da Vinci to the impressionists and everything in between. The building is stunning as well, so be sure to look up while you are exploring.

National Maritime Museum

Romney Rd, SE10 9NF Greenwich has been home to astronomical research since the 1600s. This museum celebrates the history of navigation, maritime artwork and scientific instruments.

National Portrait Gallery

St. Martin's Pl, WC2H 0HE Portraits of royals, writers, painters, politicians and others who are of historic significance adorn the walls at this gallery.

Natural History Museum

Cromwell Rd, SW7 5BD Housed in a beautifully ornate building, this museum has a world-class collection of fossils and dinosaurs, as well as Darwin's own collection.

Royal Academy of Art

Burlington House, W1J 0BD Home of the famous Summer Exhibition, as well as rotating exhibits and permanent collections.

Science Museum

Exhibition Rd, SW7 2DD A wonderful museum to visit with kids. There is The Garden play area and The Wonderlab, as well as excellent displays covering everything from space travel to the history of medicine.

The British Library

96 Euston Rd, NW1 2DB Treasures of the British Library is a must-see for any literary lovers. You can see Shakespeare's first folio, Handel's original *Messiah*, sacred texts from around the world and much, much more. There are also rotating paid exhibits that are always beautifully done.

Tate Modern

Bankside, SE1 9TG Home to one of the largest modern art collections in the world and housed in an old Bankside power station. Head up to the viewing gallery to get sweeping views of the Thames and St Paul's Cathedral.

Tate Britain

Millbank, SW1P 4RG Home to British masterpieces and organised in a timeline. Walking through this museum shows how British art has transformed from the 1500s to the present day.

The British Museum

Great Russell St, WC1B 3DG Priceless treasures from around the world, covering thousands of years of history, have found a home here. The Elgin Marbles, Rosetta Stone, Gate of Babylon, mummies and so much more.

The Museum of London

150 London Wall, EC2Y 5HN From Roman times to present day, London's history runs parallel to the history of the United Kingdom. Highlights include Roman artifacts and the Suffragette gallery.

The Wallace Collection

Hertford House, Manchester Square, W1U 3BN This small museum is located in the heart of Marylebone and has a wonderful collection of art and antiques, as well as a lovely cafe.

Victoria and Albert Museum

Cromwell Rd, SW7 2RL This museum has a little bit of everything. Raphael Cartoons, Cast Courts, the Ardabil Carpet, sculptures, jewellery, pottery, porcelain, a splash fountain for kids to play in on a sunny day, and one of the most stunning cafes.

Windsor Castle

Hampton Court Palace

St James' Palace

Tower of London

Kensington Palace

Palace of Westminster

Banqueting House

Buckingham Palace

Kew Palace

Fulham Palace

Lambeth Palace

The Queen's House

PALACES

One of the things that makes London one of the greatest cities to visit is that it has been home to the *British Monarchy* since the time of William the Conqueror (whose reign began in 1066). The palaces of London tell the long and colourful history of this country. They are *architectural masterpieces* and house some of the country's most prized treasures. From *Windsor Castle* and the Tower of London, built by William the Conqueror, to the Tudor palaces built by Henry VIII and the relatively modern *Buckingham Palace*, London's palaces are central to the story of Britain.

These royal residencies have housed monarchs and their families over the *centuries*, and visiting them gives a glimpse into the lives they led, their triumphs and defeats – and, let's not forget, their art collections.

Palace of Westminster
SW1A 0AA (Built 1870)
The site has been home to
Parliament since the 13th century.

Windsor Castle
Windsor SL4 1NJ (Built 1070) The oldest continually occupied castle
in the world.

Tower of London
EC3N 4AB (Built 1078) Built by William the Conqueror,
it famously houses the Crown Jewels.

Lambeth Palace
SE1 7JU (Built 1435) The official London residence of
the Archbishop of Canterbury.

Hampton Court Palace
Hampton Ct Way, Molesey, KT8 9AU (Built 1514) Tudor masterpiece and
a favourite of King Henry VIII.

St James' Palace
Marlborough Rd, SW1A 1BQ (Built 1536) The official
London residence of the Prince of Wales.

Kensington Palace

Kensington Gardens, W8 4PX (Built 1605) Where Queen Victoria was born and now the Duke and Duchess of Cambridge's London residence.

The Queen's House

Romney Rd, Greater, SE10 9NF (Built 1616) Built next to the now-demolished Palace of Placentia, which was the birthplace of Henry VIII and Queen Elizabeth I.

Banqueting House

Whitehall, SW1A 2ER (Built 1619) The only surviving bit of the Palace of Whitehall. The ceiling was painted by Rubens and was completed in 1634.

Kew Palace

Royal Botanic Gardens, Richmond TW9 3AE (Built 1631) The smallest of all the royal palaces.

Buckingham Palace

SW1A 1AA (Built 1703) The first resident was Queen Victoria and it has over 700 rooms.

Fulham Palace

Bishop's Ave,
SW6 6EA (Built 1350)
The site has been a residence of the bishops of London since 704.

Elgin
Crescent

Falkland
Road

Portobello
Road

Princess
Gate Mews

Wingate
Street

Hartland
Road

Lennox
Garden
Mews

Kelly
Street

Bonny
Street

St. Luke's
Mews

Chalcot
Square

Hillgate
Street

Godfrey
Street

Westbourne
Grove

Bywater
Street

Farmer
Street

COLOURFUL LONDON

London is full of colouful streets and houses that come in every shade of the *rainbow*. From Notting Hill to Chelsea, and Camden Town to Carnaby Street, there are pockets of *brightly coloured homes* dotted throughout the capital. I always love walking by the pink house on Farmer Street that's wearing a lovely green plant as a hat, or walking down Bywater Street after some shopping on the King's Road. St Luke's Mews is so *charming* and Westbourne Park is full of not just colourful homes but charming shops and cafes as well. There is no better way to brighten up your day than a *stroll down* the colourful streets of London. While I firmly believe that these houses are to be enjoyed by everyone, please remember that people do live in them and be courteous and kind if you do take photos.

Elgin Crescent

W11 Notting Hill is one of the most colourful areas in London, and the beautiful row of houses along Elgin Crescent and Lansdowne Road are truly stunning.

Portobello Road

W11 This cheerful road is full of colourful shops and is home to the famous Portobello Market. During the week you can visit the shops, but it really comes alive at the weekend.

Westbourne Grove

W11 A few minutes' walk from Portobello Road, Westbourne Grove is full of higher-end shops, cafes, bakeries and restaurants in every colour of the rainbow.

St Luke's Mews

W11 This charming mews in Notting Hill is like something out of a fairy tale. Colourful houses, a beautiful archway draped with hanging vines and a cobbled path.

Wingate Street

W6 This colourful street is nestled between Shepherd's Bush and Hammersmith. After a stroll down the street admiring all the houses, stop in at Bears Ice Cream, which is just around the corner.

Hillgate Street

W8 Colourful houses plus delicious restaurants are to be found on Hillgate Street. Mazi is a firm favourite, and Eggbreak is a great place to go for breakfast or brunch.

Farmer Street

W8 One road over from Hillgate Street is this charming street full of perfectly pastel homes. There is also a great restaurant called Los Mochis, which serves up tacos and sushi.

Hartland Road

NW1 A stone's throw from bustling Camden Market, Hartland Road has a delightful assortment of homes in every colour of the rainbow.

Kelly Street

NW1 Tucked away in Kentish Town, this colourful street is a rainbow of pastel houses.

Bonny Street

NW1 A handful of brightly coloured homes right behind Camden Road overground. Plus there is a great coffee shop, Hidden Coffee, on the corner.

Chalcot Square

NW1 Located in the heart of Primrose Hill, this charming square is a delight to walk around. If you have little ones, there is a small playground in the park, so you can enjoy the colourful view while they play.

Falkland Road

NW5 A few minutes' walk from Kentish Town Station will lead to this brightly coloured street.

Godfrey Street

SW3 Just off the King's Road in Chelsea is this delightful street. Houses in every colour imaginable plus great shopping and restaurants nearby.

Lennox Garden Mews

SW3 Tucked between Knightsbrige and Sloane Square is this charming mews. The perfect place to explore after breakfast on Pavilion Road.

Bywater Street

SW3 This candy-coloured street just off the King's Road can't help but make you smile.

Princess Gate Mews

SW7 A handful of colourful mews streets tucked behind Exhibition Road. After you've had your fill of museums, this is a lovely place to explore.

Regent's
Park

Thames
Path

Hyde
Park

Richmond
Park

Wandle Trail
Morden

CYCLING LONDON

One of the best ways to explore London is on a
bike. There are so many lovely areas that are *bike
friendly*, and bike rentals such as Santander bikes
or Lime bikes are easily found.

I'll be honest, when I first moved to London the idea
of biking around scared me, but after getting a bike I
can't imagine London *life without it.*

These bike paths are some of my favourites in the city
and offer *beautiful scenery* along bike-friendly roads.

Hyde Park

W2 The cycle paths take you past Kensington Palace, the Albert Memorial or along the Serpentine. A great place to rent bikes if you want to explore the whole park.

Richmond Park

TW10 Wild fields, local deer and wildflowers – cycling here feels like you are a world away from London.

Thames Path

Across London from Hampton Court to Greenwich The perfect route for sightseeing. You could bike all the way from Kew Gardens to Greenwich and see almost every major London landmark.

Wandle Trail Morden

SM4 A long path that takes you from central London to Croydon following the path of the river Wandle. There are parks and cafes along the way, as well as greenery and wildlife.

Your Neighbourhood

Cycling is a great way to explore your local area, whether you live there or are visiting. Most bike rides I take are within 2 miles of my flat – usually to the local bakery for some bread or a treat!

Regent's Park London

NW1
Perfect for a leisurely ride or, weather permitting, a picnic with friends.

Wellcome Collection

Alan Turing Blue Plaque

ALAN TURING 1912-1954 Code-breaker and Pioneer of Computer Science was born here

CHARLES DARWIN 1809-1882 Naturalist lived in a house on this site 1838-1842

Benjamin Franklin House

Charles Darwin Blue Plaque

FLEMING DISCOVERED PENICILLIN

Alexander Fleming Museum

LCC SIR ISAAC NEWTON 1662-1727 Lived Here

Isaac Newton Blue Plaques

Trafalgar Square

Royal Observator Greenwich

ROSALIND FRANKLIN 1920-1958 Pioneer of the study of molecular structures including DNA lived here 1951-1958

Science Museum

Natural History Museum

Burlington House

Michael Faraday Memorial

Florence Nightingale Museum

Rosalind Franklin Blue Plaque

SCIENTIFIC LONDON

Some of the world's most famous scientists have called London home. From *Newton to Darwin* and *Franklin to Fleming*, the discoveries and advancements to science that have been made in the nation's capital are countless.

If you are looking to learn about science with young ones, a visit to one of the many *science-based museums* is a great day out. For those who are lifelong learners, the many different scientific societies offer public lectures discussing latest *discoveries*, and the history of science can be found scattered around London, be it the Broad Street pump, the imperial measures of Trafalgar Square, or the monuments, statues and plaques to the great men and women who *dedicated their life* to scientific discoveries and exploration.

Science Museum

Exhibition Rd, SW7 2DD

With interactive displays and hands-on exhibits, this is a great place for kids and adults alike.

Natural History Museum

Cromwell Rd, SW7 5BD

This museum houses an unparalleled collection of animals, plants, rocks and fossils. Say hello to the Darwin statue as you make your way up the grand stairs.

Wellcome Collection

183 Euston Rd, NW1 2BE

A wonderful collection of medical antiques, along with rotating exhibits exploring what it truly means to be human.

Royal Observatory Greenwich

Blackheath Ave, SE10 8XJ

The birthplace of time as we know it today. You can explore the scientific instruments used by astronomers of old, or see a star show in the planetarium.

Alexander Fleming Museum

135A Praed St, W2 1RN

Explore this laboratory-turned-museum where famed scientist Alexander Fleming discovered penicillin in 1928.

Charles Darwin Blue Plaque

115 Gower St, WC1E 6AP

Darwin was a naturalist, and his extensive research on plants and animals led to significant discoveries into the mechanisms of evolution.

Alan Turing Blue Plaque

2 Warrington Cres, W9 1ER

Enjoy a walk around the neighbourhood where Alan Turing, codebreaker and inventor of computer science, was born.

Rosalind Franklin Blue Plaque

Donovan Court, 107 Drayton Gardens, SW10 9QS

Franklin's skill as an X-ray crystallographer helped lead to the discovery of the structure of DNA.

Florence Nightingale Museum

2 Lambeth Palace Rd, SE1 7EW

This museum celebrates the life and achievements of Florence Nightingale, who is considered the founder of modern nursing.

Michael Faraday Memorial

Elephant and Castle, SE1 6TG

This memorial honours one of the fathers of electricity. His discoveries have helped advance every aspect of science.

Isaac Newton Blue Plaques

87 Jermyn St, SW1Y 6JD

One of the most influential scientists. He was the creator of classical mechanics and calculus. He also developed the laws of motion and was able to quantify gravity.

Benjamin Franklin House

36 Craven St, WC2N 5NF

One of the founding fathers of America spent over 15 years living in London. His scientific work was extensive, and he is known as one of the fathers of electricity.

Trafalgar Square

WC2N 5DN

The markers on the stairs were installed to preserve the measurements, after the original standards of measure were lost in a fire at the houses of parliament.

Burlington House

Burlington House, W1J 0BQ

Home to scientific societies including the Royal Astronomical Society. Each society hosts events including public lectures and family days.

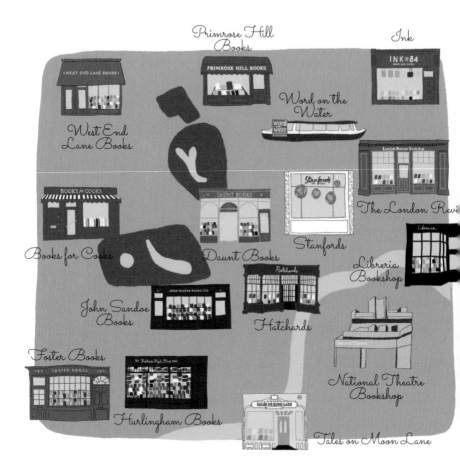

Primrose Hill
Books

Ink

West End
Lane Books

Word on the
Water

Books for Cooks

Daunt Books

Stanfords

The London Revi

Libreria
Bookshop

John Sandoe
Books

Hatchards

Foster Books

National Theatre
Bookshop

Hurlingham Books

Tales on Moon Lane

BOOKSHOPS

Bookshops are my happy place. I love walking through the aisles, looking at *tables covered with books* and reading the shelves full of staff recommendations. I've spent countless afternoons *browsing* my favourite bookshops, and I'm always staying up past my bedtime reading my way through my endless 'to-read' list. When I go on holiday I always keep an eye out for bookshops no matter what country we are in, which has led me to buying children's books in Japanese simply because they were *beautifully illustrated*, and a second-hand copy of 'Pride and Prejudice' because I had left my copy at home when we were visiting the Peak District. London is full of top-tier bookshops *specialising in everything* from cookbooks to travel books. There is no better way, in my opinion, to get a feel for London than to explore them.

West End Lane Books

277 W End Ln, NW6 1QS A charming local bookstore with an assortment of events and a great selection of books.

Primrose Hill Books

134 Regent's Park Rd, NW1 8XL Located in darling Primrose Hill, this shop carries a great selection of new and second-hand books.

Word on the Water

Regent's Canal Towpath, N1C 4LW The floating book barge with events, a fun selection of books and, if you time it right, live jazz music.

The London Review

14–16 Bury Pl, WC1A 2JL Located in the heart of Bloomsbury, this bookshop is wonderfully curated. They also have a podcast, host events and have a great cafe as well.

Daunt Books

Multiple locations across London The Marybelone location is one of the most stunning bookshops in London. Half the store is dedicated to travel books, and the rest is a wonderful selection of books from every genre.

Ink

84 Highbury Park, N5 2XE A charming independent bookshop hosting events and workshops and is a favourite among North London locals.

Libreria Bookshop

65 Hanbury St, E1 5JP A modern bookshop with a wonderful selection of books stacked to the ceiling.

Huringham Books

91 Fulham High St, SW6 3JS Boasting an amazing selection of used books, you'll definitely be able to find your next good read here.

Fosters Books

183 Chiswick High Rd, W4 2DR This beautiful shop in Chiswick specialises in rare and out-of-print books.

Stanfords

7 Mercer Walk, WC2H 9FA If you need a travel book, this is the place to go. It's full of guides, maps and travel writing from every corner of the planet. Whether you're planning your next trip or just want to armchair travel, this is the perfect place to stock up.

National Theatre Bookshop

National Theatre, SE1 9PX Outside, the South Bank hosts a huge array of second-hand booksellers, but if you find yourself looking for plays or a uniquely curated bookstore, pop into the National Theatre and browse their wonderful collection.

Hatchards

187 Piccadilly, W1J 9LE The UK's oldest bookstore. They often have signed copies of new releases, and be sure to check out their great list of their favourite 200 novels of the past 200 years.

John Sandoe Books

10 Blacklands Terrace, SW3 2SR Full of interesting books and the most knowledgeable staff, so you are bound to find a book to take home.

Books for Cooks

4 Blenheim Cres, W11 1NN A shop entirely devoted to amazing cookbooks. If you need cooking inspiration, this shop in Notting Hill is the place to go. They also do a set lunch which is amazing. Check out their Twitter for info.

Tales on Moon Lane

25 Half Moon Ln, SE24 9JU A dream of a children's bookshop in South London.

Paddington
Recreation Ground

Victoria
Park

Platform 9 ¾

HOGWARTS EXPRESS

London
Zoo

Diana
Memorial
Playground

Little Angel
Theatre

Holland
Park
Adventure
Playground

London Transport
Museum

Greenwich
Park

Science
Museum

Tate Modern

National Maritime
Museum

Natural History
Museum

Victoria
and Albert
Museum

Battersea Park

LONDON WITH KIDS

London is full of wonderful places to explore with young kids, you just need to know where to look. From *world-class* playgrounds and splash pads in iconic locations to enthralling *museum exhibits* and West End shows. You can truly tailor your trip to your *family's interests* because there is something fun for *kids of all ages*, and for all budgets, in London.

If you are traveling with young kids *my advice* would be don't overdo it. Planning *one or two activities* or attractions a day is more than enough, and then make sure you set aside time to play in London's beautiful *parks and gardens.*

Paddington Recreation Ground
Randolph Ave, W9 1PD

A charming playground featuring a mini colourful row of houses.

Holland Park Adventure Playground
55 Abbotsbury Rd, W14 8EL

A large playground with several different areas to explore, your kids won't want to leave.

Diana Memorial Playground
Kensington Gardens, Broad Walk, W2 4RU

A truly magical playground. The main feature is a giant pirate ship.

Battersea Park
SW11 4NJ

This park boasts a mini zoo and a great playground, as well as a boating lake and beautiful gardens.

Greenwich Park
SE10 8XG

A maritime-themed playground is located in the northern corner of the park, or visit the planetarium and see a star show.

Victoria Park
Grove Rd, E3 5TB

Multiple playgrounds are spread across this park, including a splash pad and, skate park.

Science Museum
Exhibition Rd, SW7 2DD

Beyond the exhibits, The Garden in the basement is perfect for little ones and The Wonderlab offers up interactive activities for kids aged seven and older.

Natural History Museum
Cromwell Rd, SW7 5BD

Explore exhibits on dinosaurs and extinct animals and learn about our Earth's history.

Victoria and Albert Museum

Cromwell Rd, SW7 2RL

The inner courtyard has one the most picturesque paddling fountains in London.

Tate Modern

Bankside, SE1 9TG

A very child-friendly museum with wonderful activities and ideas to help kids learn about art.

National Maritime Museum

Romney Rd, SE10 9NF

Let your young ones explore and play in the Ahoy! Gallery, walk on a giant map of the globe or pick up a family trail to explore the collections.

London Transport Museum

The Piazza, WC2E 7BB

Featuring two play areas as well as lots of fun areas and activities to explore, this museum is a family favourite.

Little Angel Theatre

14 Dagmar Passage, N1 2DN

A charming theatre with puppet shows for children and families. They have shows for kids age two and up.

Platform 9 ¾

N1 9AP

A must-visit for all Harry Potter lovers. The perfect place to take your photo right before you board the Hogwarts Express.

ZSL London Zoo

Outer Cir, London NW1 4RY

Conservation and research is at the heart of this zoo, making it a fun and educational day out for the family.

Emmeline & Christabel Pankhurst's home

Elizabeth Garrett Anderson's home

Millicent Fawcett's home

Hertha Ayrton's home

VOTES for WOMEN
COME
TO THE
HOUSE OF
COMMONS
at 7.30 pm

COURAGE
CALLS TO
COURAGE
EVERYWHERE

Suffragette Demonstration, Trafalgar Square

Women's Sunday, Hyde Park

W.P.U.
DEEDS
NOT
WORDS
VOTES FOR WOMEN

Charlotte Marsh

Millicent Fawcett statue

VOTES FOR WOMEN

Annie Kenny

Christabel Pankhurst

Emmeline & Christabel Pankhurst Memorial

SUFFRAGETTE LONDON

Women's suffrage started long before the early 1900s. Women had been *campaigning* throughout the proceeding decades for the right to vote, but no progress was made. This all changed at the turn of the century when the *Suffragettes* decided that they would *not take no* for an answer. This Suffragette London illustration highlights the women and events that were critical to furthering *women's rights* in the United Kingdom. These women are celebrated today as the *trailblazers* that brought about a start to equality with voting rights.

Emmeline & Christabel Pankhurst's Home

50 Clarendon Road, Notting Hill, W11 3AD

Emmeline and Christabel Pankhurst were a mother and daughter who worked hand-in-hand to further the cause of the Women's Social and Political Union (WSPU), which promoted the motto 'Deeds not Words'. Christabel was made a dame in 1936 for her public and social services.

Emmeline & Christabel Pankhurst Memorial

Victoria Tower Gardens Millbank, SW1P 3JA

There is no doubt that the actions of Emmeline and Christabel, mother and daughter, paved the way for women to be granted the right to vote.

Hertha Ayrton's home

41 Norfolk Square – inventor, physicist, mathematician, suffragette

Hertha attended Cambridge University, where she studied mathematics, but at the time Cambridge did not grant degrees to women. She sat her exams at University College London and in 1881 was granted a Bachelor of Science. Hertha went on to study physics and engineering and was awarded the Hughes Medal from the Royal Society in 1906 for her research into the electric arc.

Elizabeth Garrett Anderson's home

20 Upper Berkeley Street – physician, suffragette

In 1865 Elizabeth was the first woman to qualify as a physician and surgeon. Elizabeth opened her own practice and co-founded the London School of Medicine for Women. In 1908 Elizabeth was elected mayor of Aldeburgh and became the first female mayor in England.

Millicent Fawcett's home

2 Gower Street – writer, activist, suffragette

Millicent was a campaigner for women obtaining an education. She wrote several books on politics and women's rights. She believed that words, reason and debate would be sufficient to help progress the rights of women. Millicent became the leader of the National Union of Women's Suffrage Societies (NUWSS), which was the largest suffragette group in Britain.

Suffragette demonstration led by Sylvia Pankhurst

Trafalgar Square, 27 July 1913

This was an iconic protest which Sylvia Pankhurst led and spoke at, encouraging the crowd to march on Downing Street. Sylvia had been arrested the previous month for 'disturbing the peace'; she was arrested again at this demonstration.

Millicent Fawcett statue

Parliament Square

This was the first statue of a woman in Parliament Square. It was unveiled on the 100th anniversary of women obtaining the right to vote in 2018. Statues in this square are reserved for statesmen and notable individuals, and its location across from Parliament is a rallying point for protests and marches.

Women's Sunday

Hyde Park, 21 June 1908

A monumental protest in the history of women's right to the vote. Over 500,000 people were in attendance and, at the time, it was the largest-ever demonstration in the UK.

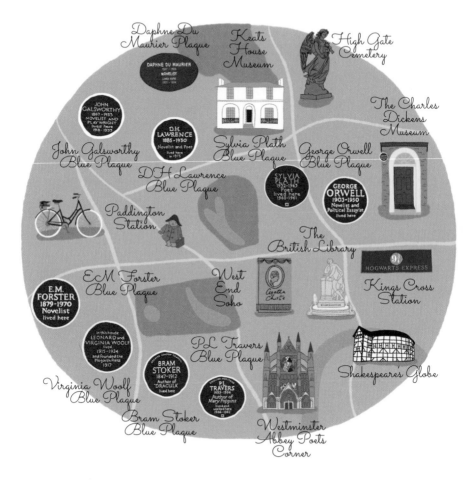

Daphne Du Maurier Plaque

DAPHNE DU MAURIER
NOVELIST
LIVED HERE
1933-1936

Keats House Museum

High Gate Cemetery

JOHN GALSWORTHY
1867-1933
NOVELIST AND PLAYWRIGHT
lived here 1918-1933

D.H. LAWRENCE
1885-1930
Novelist and Poet
lived here in 1915

The Charles Dickens Museum

John Galsworthy Blue Plaque

Sylvia Plath Blue Plaque

George Orwell Blue Plaque

DH Lawrence Blue Plaque

SYLVIA PLATH
1932-1963
Poet
lived here
1960-1961

GEORGE ORWELL
1903-1950
Novelist and Political Essayist
lived here

Paddington Station

The British Library

E.M. FORSTER
1879-1970
Novelist
lived here

EM Forster Blue Plaque

West End Soho

HOGWARTS EXPRESS

Kings Cross Station

In this house LEONARD and VIRGINIA WOOLF lived 1915-1924 and founded the Hogarth Press 1917

BRAM STOKER
1847-1912
Author of 'DRACULA'
lived here

PL Travers Blue Plaque

Virginia Woolf Blue Plaque

Bram Stoker Blue Plaque

P.L. TRAVERS
1899-1996
Author of Mary Poppins
Lived and worked here
1946-1962

Shakespeare's Globe

Westminster Abbey Poets Corner

LITERARY LONDON

London has influenced writers for centuries. The invention of the printing press in the 1400s enabled *books to be published* and mass produced, making it feasible for more than just the ultra-wealthy to read. From *Chaucer*, whose books have never been out of print since the 1400s, to the modern writers of today, London has captured many authors' hearts and plays a *prominent* role in English literature.

When I am out walking, I love noticing the plaques and monuments that commemorate these authors and poets. It's thrilling to think about *P. L. Travers* walking down the King's Road, *Virginia Woolf* meeting up with friends in Bloomsbury, or Shakespeare crossing London Bridge to get to the Globe Theatre. The places we live *influence* who we are, and I created this map to celebrate the authors who called London their home.

Daphne du Maurier Plaque
3 Well Rd, NW3 1LJ
Her books include classics such as *The Birds* and *Rebecca*.

John Galsworthy Blue Plaque
5 Admiral's Walk, NW3 6RR
Galsworthy notably wrote *The Forsyte Saga*, for which he received a Nobel Prize.

D. H. Lawrence Blue Plaque
1 Byron Villas, Vale of Health, NW3 1AR
Author of *Lady Chatterley's Lover* and *Sons and Lovers*.

E. M. Forster Blue Plaque
Arlington Park Mansions, Sutton Lane, W4 4HE
A Room with a View, *Howards End* and *A Passage to India* are well-loved classics.

Virginia Woolf Blue Plaque
29 Fitzroy Square, W1T 6LQ
Modernist author of *Mrs Dalloway* and *A Room of One's Own*.

Bram Stoker Blue Plaque
19 St Leonard's Terrace, SW3 4QG
Best known for the Gothic classic *Dracula*.

PL Travers Blue Plaque
50 Smith St, SW3 4EP
Creator of the Mary Poppins series.

Westminster Abbey Poets' Corner
20 Deans Yd, SW1P 3PA
Graves of Chaucer, Dickens, Hardy and more, along with memorials to dozens of other writers.

The Globe
21 New Globe Walk, SE1 9DT
There is nothing quite like seeing a Shakespeare play in this re-built theatre.

West End Soho

Covent Garden, Piccadilly

From Agatha Christie to J. K. Rowling, there are shows for everyone.

Paddington Station

W2 1HB

Visit a statue of everyone's favourite bear at the station.

Sylvia Plath Blue Plaque

3 Chalcot Square, NW1 8YB

Poet and writer of *The Colossus* and *The Bell Jar*.

Keats House

10 Keats Grove, NW3 2RR

The former home and museum of the Romantic poet John Keats.

George Orwell

Blue Plaque 50 Lawford Road, NW5 2LN

Best known for *Animal Farm* and *1984*.

Kings Cross Station

King's Cross, Euston Rd, N1C 4AX

A visit to Platform 9¾ is a must for any Harry Potter fans.

The British Library

96 Euston Rd, NW1 2DB

An incredible collection of manuscripts, books and letters.

The Charles Dickens Museum

48-49 Doughty St, WC1N 2LX

Celebrating his novels and showing how his life would have been.

Highgate Cemetery

Swain's Ln, N6 6PJ

The final resting places of many famous writers, including Douglas Adams and Karl Marx.

LONDON

BY SEASON

PART FOUR

ROMANTIC LONDON + LONDON IN SPRING

HOT CROSS BUNS + LONDON IN SUMMER + LONDON IN AUTUMN

+ HAUNTED LONDON + MINCE PIES + FESTIVE LONDON

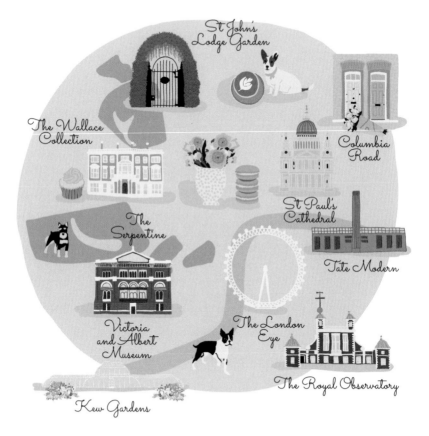

St John's
Lodge Garden

The Wallace
Collection

Columbia
Road

The
Serpentine

St Paul's
Cathedral

Tate Modern

Victoria
and Albert
Museum

The London
Eye

The Royal Observatory

Kew Gardens

ROMANTIC LONDON

There are so many ways we can show our love for others.
It might be a kind word, offering a *helping hand*, a
fancy dinner, a gift or a hug. There is no one way to be
romantic, and I created this map to showcase some of
the best non-traditionally romantic things to do in London.
These places are the *perfect spot* to take anyone
you love, be it your sweetheart, your best friend or
your furry friend.

Kew Gardens

Kew, Richmond, TW9 3AE
Refresh the soul as you wonder though these beautiful gardens and see plants from all over the world.

St John's Lodge Garden

Regent's Park Inner Cir, NW1 4NR A hidden garden in Regent's Park that feels like you've stepped into a magical world. Stroll through this beautiful garden and bonus points if you bring treats to share.

The Wallace Collection

Hertford House, W1U 3BN This small and cosy museum is full of treasures. Perfect for walking hand-in-hand with your favourite person. Stop for tea and cake in their pink cafe.

The Serpentine

Hyde Park W2 2AR Head to Hyde Park for a romantic stroll along the Serpentine and enjoy the Italian Gardens and gorgeous views as you walk.

Victoria and Albert Museum

Cromwell Rd, SW7 2RL Check out their amazing jewellery collection and pick which crown you would wear.

The London Eye

South Bank, SE1 7PB For those who love a romantic view, nothing compares to the London Eye for sweeping vistas in every direction. It is extra beautiful if you time your ride for sunset.

The Royal Observatory

Blackheath Ave, SE10 8XJ Enjoy a star show, take in the views of London and ponder the meaning of time.

Tate Modern

Bankside, SE1 9TG Head to the viewing galleries to take in sweeping views of the Thames or wander through the building and discuss art with your favourite person.

St Paul's Cathedral

St Paul's Churchyard, EC4M 8AD Climb to the whispering gallery and whisper sweet nothings to your loved one.

Columbia Road

Columbia Rd, E2 7RG
Take a Sunday stroll though one of the loveliest flower markets and pick a bunch of truly unique blooms for the love in your life.

The Hill
Gardens and
Pergola

Highgate
Woods

St John's
Lodge Gardens

Notting Hill

Chelsea

Queen Mary's
Rose Gardens

St James'
Park

St Paul's
Cathedral

Hyde
Park

Holland
Park

Fulham
Palace

Greenwich
Park

Kew
Gardens

Battersea
Park

Hampton
Court

Richmond
Park

LONDON IN SPRING

LONDON BY SEASON

Spring is a welcome reprieve from the dark winter days. Blossoms start popping up in *February*, bringing much-needed *colour and cheer*, and London has some of the most exquisite gardens to enjoy these blooms. From February until the end of the summer, blossoms can be found in *every corner* of London. Daffodils and magnolia blossoms are the first hint of spring, followed by camellias, cherry blossoms, tulips, wisteria and finally *roses*. Houses draped in wisteria, *English rose gardens*, carpets of daffodils and pink cherry blossoms are some of the delights to behold in London in the spring.

Notting Hill

W11
Magnolia, wisteria,
cherry blossoms.

St James's Park

SW1A Daffodils, tulips, cherry blossoms and planted beds.

Holland Park

W8 6LU Wisteria, roses and tulips.

Hyde Park

W2 2UD Roses, cherry blossoms.

Kew Gardens

Kew, Richmond, TW9 3AE Everything! Daffodils, wisteria,
cherry blossoms, roses, planted beds and more.

Hampton Court

Hampton Ct Way, Molesey, East Molesey KT8 9AU
Roses, planted beds.

Queen Mary's Rose Gardens

Chester Rd, NW1 4NR Roses and wisteria.

St John's Lodge Gardens

Regent's Park Inner Cir, NW1 4NR Roses, wisteria, planted beds.

The Hill Gardens and Pergola

The Pergola, Inverforth Cl, NW3 7EX Wisteria, roses.

Fulham Palace
Bishop's Ave, SW6 6EA Truly epic wisteria.

 ### Greenwich Park
SE10 8XH Cherry blossoms, roses.

Highgate Woods
Muswell Hill Rd, N10 3JN Bluebells.

Richmond Park
Richmond Park, Richmond TW10 5HS Rhododendrons, azaleas.

 ### St Paul's Cathedral
St. Paul's Churchyard, EC4M 8AD Cherry blossoms.

Battersea Park
SW11 4NJ Cherry blossoms.

Chelsea
SW3 Cherry blossoms, magnolia, wisteria, Chelsea Flower Show, Chelsea in Bloom.

Here is when to keep an eye out for each type of spring blossoms

FEBRUARY to MARCH:
Magnolia, daffodils

MARCH:
Camellias

MARCH to EARLY MAY:
Cherry blossoms

APRIL:
Tulips

APRIL:
Azalea and rhododendrons

APRIL to JUNE:
Wisteria

JUNE:
Roses

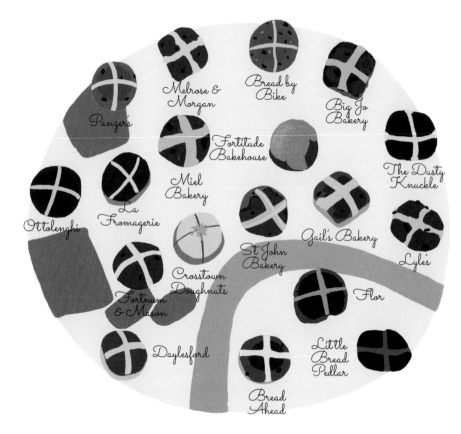

Panzer's

Melrose &
Morgan

Bread by
Bike

Big Jo
Bakery

Fortitude
Bakehouse

The Dusty
Knuckle

Miel
Bakery

Ottolenghi

La
Fromagerie

Gail's Bakery

Lyle's

Crosstown
Doughnuts

St John
Bakery

Flor

Fortnum
& Mason

Daylesford

Little
Bread
Pedlar

Bread
Ahead

HOT CROSS BUNS

In the weeks preceding Easter, bakeries start to fill with hot cross buns. Hot cross buns have been around for *hundreds of years* – by some accounts, since the 14th century – and their tradition *lives on* today. They were traditionally eaten to mark the end of Lent, with the *cross on the top* representing the crucifixion of Christ. The original HCB is made with dried fruit, orange and spices mixed into the dough, but these days you can find lots of different *varieties and versions.* Whether you are looking for traditional or a bit more avant-garde, there is something to please everyone.

Gail's Bakery

Multiple locations across London So delicious, and you can also try their HCB pudding – hot cross buns soaked with vanilla custard, smoked bacon and maple syrup.

Panzer's Deli

13–19 Circus Rd, NW8 6PB It might be hard to decide between their HCBs and bagels. Best to get both!

Bread Ahead

Multiple locations across London So yummy and fluffy, with the nicest glaze.

La Fromagerie

Multiple locations, Marylebone, Bloomsbury, Highbury Grab some HCBs while stocking up on your Easter cheese.

Ottolenghi

Multiple locations across London Delicious buns of yumminess.

Fortnum & Mason

181 Piccadilly, St James's, W1A 1ER Offering up a variety of unique HCB flavours.

Daylesford

Multiple locations, Notting Hill, Chelsea, Marylebone, Belgravia Eat them toasted with butter for the ultimate treat.

Crosstown Doughnuts

Multiple locations across London A HCB doughnut!

Miel Bakery

57 Warren St, W1T 5NR Citrus and spice and everything nice.

Melrose and Morgan

Multiple locations, Primrose Hill, Hampstead A lovely traditional HCB.

Bread by Bike

30 Brecknock Rd, N7 0DD Packed with fruit and spices.

Fortitude Bakehouse

35 Colonnade, WC1N 1JA Spiced Easter buns that are fluffy and delicious.

Big Jo Bakery

324 Hornsey Rd, N7 7HE Full of candied citrus and spices.

The Dusty Knuckle

Abbot St, E8 3DP Perfectly spiced and delicious.

Lyle's London Tea Building

56 Shoreditch High St, E1 6JJ Spices and fruit in balanced harmony.

St John Bakery

3 Neal's Yard, Seven Dials, WC2H 9DP Classic buns baked to perfection.

Flor Bakery

Voyager Estate South 6, Spa Rd, SE16 4RP The flavour sings in their buns.

Little Bread Pedlar

Spa Terminus, Dockley Rd, SE16 3FJ
Best to order in advance as they can sell out quickly.

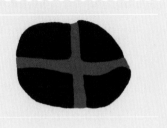

Primrose
Hill

Hampstead
Heath

Paddington Recreation
Ground

Regent's
Park

Victoria
Park

Holland Park

Hyde Park

Battersea Park

Crystal
Palace

Richmond
Park

Clapham
Common

LONDON IN SUMMER

I love the saying 'There's no such thing as bad weather, only unsuitable clothing', because being outside is *integral* to London life. This is even more true in the summer. On warm days the parks will be full of *families picnicking*, kids playing, friends catching up and sunbathers.

London has so many *beautiful parks* and they all have unique characteristics. From Royal Parks to old hunting grounds, you can find *wild deer*, woodland walks, beautiful *English gardens*, bathing ponds and ice cream trucks.

Victoria Park

E3
Lovely playground, splash
pool, gardens and a
Chinese pagoda.

Hampstead Heath

NW3 The bathing ponds, Kenwood House, views of London
and woodland trails.

Primrose Hill

NW1 A lovely view of London from the top of the hill with
nice cafes nearby.

Paddington Recreation Ground

Randolph Ave, W9 1PD The cutest kids' playground,
tennis courts and a rose garden.

Holland Park

Holland Park Ave, W11 4UA Amazing playgrounds, beautiful
Japanese garden, English gardens and peacocks!

Hyde Park

W2 There is so much to explore here, from the Italian Gardens,
Kensington Palace, the Serpentine lido, boating on the Serpentine
and the Serpentine Gallery to amazing playgrounds, lovely cafes,
statues and memorials.

Richmond Park

Richmond TW10 5HS Wild deer, bike paths and the stunning Isabella Plantation.

Battersea Park

SW11 4NJ Lovely playgrounds, a children's zoo and the Peace Pergola.

Clapham Common

SW4 Open and spacious park that's great for running and picnics.

Crystal Palace

SE19 Victorian-era dinosaur trail and hedge maze.

Regent's Park

NW1
Lots of areas to explore, including London Zoo, Queen Mary's Rose Garden, St John's Lodge Garden, a handful of playgrounds, a boating lake and English gardens.

Regent's
Canal

Regent's
Park

Hampstead

Hyde
Park

Barbican

Holland
Park

Chelsea

St James'
Park

Greenwich
Park

Kew
Gardens

Richmond Park

Hever Castle
& Gardens

LONDON IN AUTUMN

LONDON BY SEASON

London can get overlooked in the autumn, but there are *stunning places* to be found as summer fades. The leaves generally start turning in September, making October the peak time to experience autumn in London.

There are *vibrant trees*, houses draped with Virginia creeper and *crunchy leaves* to stomp through. Autumn colours are in abundance if you take the time to look and it is the perfect season to walk, with a *warm drink* in hand, around your favourite neighbourhoods to see what colourful delights you discover.

Hampstead

NW3

Hampstead is a wonderful area to explore in the autumn. From the leaf-covered house on Fitzjohn's Avenue to the autumnal-coloured trees on the Heath (not to mention the many cosy pubs).

Richmond Park

Richmond TW10 5HS For stunning autumn foliage, Richmond Park is a wonderful place to wander round. The Isabella Plantation has a large variety of trees showing off bright colours.

Regent's Canal

Kings Cross to Little Venice The trees lining Regent's Canal set a beautiful scene from Paddington all the way to Victoria Park.

Regent's Park

NW1 For lovely autumnal foliage, check out St John's Lodge Garden and The Broad Walk.

Hyde Park

W2 Walk along the Serpentine to see some of the best autumn colours.

Greenwich Park

SE10 Avenues of trees lead to sweeping views of the Thames, the Old Royal Naval College in one direction and the Greenwich Royal Observatory in the other.

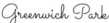

Chelsea

SW3 One of the most photographed places in London in autumn is Kynance Mews. The stunning display of red leaves draping over the archway is beautiful.

Holland Park

Holland Park Ave, W11 4UA The Kyoto Gardens in particular are stunning as there leaves change.

Kew Gardens

Kew, Richmond, TW9 3AE With thousands of species of plants, autumn is just as vibrant as any spring or summer at Kew.

St James's Park

SW1A A stunning display of autumn foliage with iconic backdrops of Buckingham Palace and Horse Guards Parade.

Barbican

EC2Y 8DS Autumn foliage amidst brutalist architecture makes a walk around the Barbican a perfect activity at this time of year.

Hever Castle & Gardens

Hever Rd, Hever, Edenbridge TN8 7NG Located just outside of London, Hever Castle is stunning in autumn. In October the ivy covering the castle turns vibrant red, making it the perfect place to visit during the autumn months.

Hampstead
Heath

Highgate
Cemetery

Hampstead
Parish Church

The Wellcome
Collection

Regent's
Park

The Crypt
Gallery

Charter House
Square

Paddington
Old Cemetery

The Cafe in
the Crypt

Liverpool
Street

Hampton
Court

Hyde Park
Pet Cemetery

IN
LOVING
MEMORY OF
MUFFIN
AGED 15 YEARS

Sir John Soane's
Museum

Tower of
London

Westminster
Abbey

Brompton
Cemetery

Nunhead
Cemetery

HAUNTED LONDON

A city as old as London is bound to have haunted corners and spooky settings – you just need to know where to look. From historic palaces with *torrid pasts* to crypts tuned into art galleries and cafes, the city is full of things that feel a bit eerie.

London has also been the *inspiration* for Gothic tales and ghost stories. *The Strange Case of Dr Jekyll and Mr Hyde, The Picture of Dorian Gray* and *Dracula* are all set in a Gothic London.

So whether you want to explore a Victorian pet cemetery, eat dinner in a crypt or picnic on the grounds of a former plague pit, London leaves you *spoiled for choice* when it comes to things that are a bit sinister.

The Cafe in the Crypt

St Martin in the Fields, Trafalgar Sq, WC2N 4JH Exactly what its name describes, this is a cafe in the crypt of the church. It is a hauntingly beautiful setting for a cafe. With tables and chairs scraping over old headstones and low arched ceilings, you can enjoy a spooky setting while also having a delicious meal or dessert.

The Crypt Gallery

165 Euston Rd, NW1 2BA A crypt turned into an art gallery. This crypt was used for coffin burials, which have now all been removed, leaving a wonderful, if slightly creepy, exhibition space.

Hyde Park Pet Cemetery

41 Bayswater Rd, W2 4RQ Located behind the lodge at Victoria Gate is a hidden pet cemetery. Dating back to the Victorian era, over 1,000 pets have been buried here. It is rarely open to the public and can only be accessed by guided tour.

Highgate Cemetery

Swain's Ln, N6 6PJ Highgate Cemetery boasts some of the most beautiful gravestones and monuments in London. The abundance of trees and overgrown hedges add to the spooky atmosphere.

Paddington Old Cemetery

Willesden Ln, NW6 7SD This cemetery has a beautiful chapel that is slowly falling into disrepair. Keep an eye out for the honey bees as there is an apiary on the grounds where Tombstone Honey is produced.

Brompton Cemetery

Fulham Rd, SW10 9UG This Grade I-listed cemetery has a stunningly beautiful chapel and rich history. Walk the pathways and enjoy the wildlife and greenery.

Tower of London

London EC3N 4AB Thought to be haunted by Guy Fawkes, Lady Jane Grey, Henry VI, and Anne Boleyn.

Westminster Abbey

20 Deans Yd, SW1P 3PA This is the final resting ground for 17 British monarchs and a Gothic masterpiece. Filled with almost a century of history, it is a must-visit place.

The Graveyard at Hampstead Parish Church

Church Row, NW3 6UU In *Dracula*, this was where the undead Lucy Westenra was placed in her vault by Van Helsing and Dr Seward. It is not hard to imagine vampires walking through this graveyard, with its overgrown corners and weathered tombs.

The Wellcome Collection

183 Euston Rd, NW1 2BE One of London's spookier museums. Its collection explores some gruesome medical history and human nature. The gift shop here is also worth checking out.

Sir John Soane's Museum

13 Lincoln's Inn Fields, WC2A 3BP This museum feels like you are walking into the magical world of Harry Potter. John Soane's collection has remained almost untouched in the 180 years since his death and is an eclectic assortment of sculptures, art, a memorial to the family dog and the sarcophagus of the Egyptian Pharaoh Seti I.

Hampton Court

Hampton Ct Way, Molesey, East Molesey KT8 9AU Hampton Court has several resident ghosts, one of them being Catherine Howard, Henry VIII's fifth wife.

Liverpool Street / Charter House Square

Barbican, EC1M When you wander round the modern shops and streets, remember that once, both of these were plague pits.

Nunhead Cemetery

Linden Grove, SE15 3LP This Victorian cemetery is also a nature reserve, perfect for beautifully spooky walks.

Gail's

Margot
Bakery

Jolene

Pophams

Ottolenghi

Boxcar
Baker

Miel
Bakery

Holborn
Dining
Room

The Lily
Vanilli Bakery

Paul A Young

Bread Ahead

Fortnum &
Mason

Flor
Bakery

St John
Bakery

Hotel Chocolat

Little Bread Pedlar

MINCE PIES

A sure sign that the Christmas season is upon us is when mince pies start to pop up in shops and bakeries. Mince pies have been a *Christmas* mainstay since the 13th century. Even though the recipe has changed over time, the general idea is the same – dried fruit soaked in *brandy and spices,* wrapped up in a crumbly pastry crust. Enjoyed throughout the holiday season and a *favourite treat* of Father Christmas, mince pies are the quintessential seasonal treat.

Boxcar Baker

→ **7A Wyndham Pl, W1H 1PN**
Scrumptious pies served
in a lovely location.

Bread Ahead
Multiple locations across London Traditional pies full of flavour.

Flor Bakery
Voyager Estate South 6, Spa Rd, SE16 4RP Crumbly and
spiced to perfection.

Fortnum & Mason
181 Piccadilly, St James's, W1A 1ER Classic mince pies
boxed up and ready to go.

Gail's
Multiple locations across London Melt-in-your-mouth pastry with
a perfected spiced filling.

Holborn Dining Room
252 High Holborn, WC1V 7EN Master pastry chefs baking
up the ultimate mince pie.

Margot Bakery
121E End Rd, N2 0SZ You can taste the love that goes into making
these pies.

Jolene
Multiple locations, Shoreditch, Islington, Newton Green The filling here is wonderfully balanced with the pastry.

Little Bread Pedlar
Spa Terminus, Dockley Rd, SE16 3FJ Mince pies that people come for from all over London to enjoy.

Miel Bakery
57 Warren St, W1T 5NR Pastry encases a succulent filling that is baked to perfection.

Ottolenghi
Multiple locations across London A perfectly spiced delight.

Pophams
Multiple locations, Hackney, Islington A delicious take on the traditional mince pie.

St John Bakery
3 Neal's Yard, Seven Dials, WC2H 9DP Delightful mince pies that melt in your mouth.

Hotel Chocolat
Multiple Locations across London For those who prefer chocolate to pastry.

Paul A Young
33 Camden Passage, London N1 8EA Enjoy this master chocolatier's take on a mince pie

The Lily Vanilli Bakery
The Courtyard, 18 Ezra St, E2 7RH Flavourful mince pies served in a charming bakery.

The Nutcracker

Somerset House

Tower of London

Liberty London

Trafalgar Square

Royal Albert Hall

Natural History Museum

Fortnum & Mason

London Eye

South Bank Market

FESTIVE LONDON

Christmas time in London is simply magical. Fairy lights abound, shops are festively decorated, the air is crisp and there is *jolly music* playing everywhere. Since I moved to London, we have spent *every Christmas* here and I love it. I always invite family to come and stay because there is such a *festive atmosphere*. There are so many lovely traditions that come with the holiday season as well. Minces pies, Christmas crackers, ice skating, Brussels sprouts, yule logs, Christmas pudding, *pantomimes* and, did you know, even Christmas cards are an English invention? (The man who invented them lived in Hampstead).

If you are looking to indulge in all of the festive offerings *London* has to offer, this is the guide for you.

TIPS FOR EXPLORING LONDON

I hope you find inspiration in these illustrations. London has been a thriving city for more than a millennium and there will always be something more to explore. There is no 'right' way to explore London. The perfect trip is the trip that involves things that you find important when travelling. If you love food, make sure you plan for amazing meals. If you love a good view, make sure you see London from all the best heights. You don't need to spend a fortune to have a wonderful holiday in this city.

Here are things to think about to ensure you get the best from the city, whether you are just visiting or a dyed-in-the-wool Londoner.

1. What is important to you when you take a holiday? Are you looking to relax? Explore neighbourhoods like a local? Eat at Michelin-star restaurants? Whatever the answer to this question is, make sure you prioritise that for your trip.

2. Wear practical shoes. London is very walkable, and you can easily find yourself walking 20,000 steps a day. Londoners are practical people, so wear practical shoes.

3. Take time to enjoy the atmosphere. Make sure you sometimes put your phone and camera down and just enjoy the views and sites.

4. Walk on the right side of the pavement. Stand on the right side of the escalators. Don't stand in the middle of the pavement to check your phone.

5. Book restaurants in advance.

6. Don't try to do everything. Pick a few things and do them well. You won't be disappointed.

Go to a Christmas Concert

There are so many amazing Christmas concerts you can attend, from Handel's Messiah by Candlelight at St Martin-in-the-Fields to the King's College Choir performing carols. There is nothing quite like hearing world-class Christmas music to put you in the holiday spirit.

See The Nutcracker

Take your pick between the Royal and National Ballet.

Go Ice Skating

Somerset House, Hyde Park, Greenwich, Canary Wharf, Hampton Court ... at this time of year, all have lovely ice rinks that will get you right into the Christmas spirit, as well as provide beautiful scenery as you skate around.

Go to a Christmas Market

There are countless Christmas markets that pop up every year. South Bank Market is a favourite, but there is also Winter Wonderland, Trafalgar Square Market and so many others dotted throughout the city.

See the Decorations

Liberty London, Fortnum and Mason, Selfridges, Burlington Arcade and Marylebone High Street are always fun to walk through at Christmas time. Their window displays are delightful and are not to be missed.

See the Lights

Walk down Regent's Street, New Bond Street, Marylebone High Street, Covent Garden and Trafalgar Square to enjoy the decorations and lights.

Published in 2022 by OH Editions
Part of Welbeck Publishing Group.
Based in London and Sydney.
www.welbeckpublishing.com

Design © 2022 OH Editions

Text © 2022 Cierra Block
Illustrations © 2022 Cierra Block

A CIP catalogue record for this book is available from the British Library.

ISBN 978-1-91431-755-2

Publisher: Kate Pollard
Editor: Sophie Elletson
Desk Editor: Matt Tomlinson
Designer: Julia Murray
Illustrator: Cierra Block
Production controller: Jess Brisley
Colour reproduction: p2d

Printed and bound by RR Donnelley in China

10 9 8 7 6 5 4